Gainsborough Del.

THE RIVER TYNE, 1830.

By kind permission of Aml. Reid & Sons Ltd., from their plate.

o

A Historical Sketch

of the

Society of Friends

"IN SCORN CALLED QUAKERS"

in Newcastle and Gateshead.

1653-1898.

BY

JOHN WILLIAM STEEL,

WITH

CONTRIBUTIONS FROM OTHER FRIENDS.

To be obtained from
HEADLEY BROTHERS, BISHOPSGATE, LONDON.
THE BIBLE AND TRACT DEPOT, NEWCASTLE.
—
1899.

R. ROBINSON AND CO. LTD.,
PRINTERS,
NEWCASTLE-ON-TYNE.

Preface.

A FEW months ago a Lecture was delivered
by John William Steel, giving a historical
sketch of the Society of Friends in
Gateshead and their establishment in their
present premises in Newcastle in 1698.

Though designed only for a local audience, it was
evident to those who heard it that its preparation had
involved considerable research, and that many facts had
been collected which were worth preservation. It was
therefore suggested that the history thus commenced should
be brought down to a later date and printed.

In furtherance of this desire John William Steel
invited the assistance of other Friends whose longer
residence in Newcastle would enable them to furnish
material not at his command. The following pages are
now presented to the reader in the hope that the sketch
thus complied may not only possess some value as a local
history, but may have an interest beyond the limits of
Newcastle Friends.

It was thought that by inviting contributions from
those best able to speak from personal knowledge of the
subjects treated, the variety of style would add to the
popularity of the book. It will be seen that some of these

are of a sketchy rather than of a literary character: they are purposely given in this form in preference to attempting a more studied composition.

Voluminous manuscripts have been handed down from the correspondence and memoranda of George Richardson, which have furnished material to the Editors, who would gladly have availed themselves of similar collections representing other families, had such been at their command.

The Portraits and Silhouettes, so kindly contributed by relatives of the deceased will recall some familiar faces, and will present others to many who have known them only by tradition.

For all the help thus generously given, the Editors offer their grateful acknowledgments.

THOMAS PUMPHREY.

Summerhill Grove,
Newcastle-on-Tyne,
April, 1899.

Contents.

Index

TO BIOGRAPHICAL NOTICES AND PORTRAITS.

Index to Plans.

Key to Letters

Indicating Rooms.

A.	Meeting-house.

B.	Men's Meeting-house.

C.	Women's Meeting-house.

D.	Caretaker's House.

E.	Shops and Offices Let.

F.	Lobbies.

G.	Library and Committee Rooms.

H.	Cloak Rooms, &c.

I.	Class Rooms.

J.	General School Room.

K.	Graveyard.

L.	Vacant Ground.

M.	Entrances.

N.	Ground not then acquired.

Y.	Yard.

The Quaker of the olden time !
  How calm and firm and true,
Unspotted by its wrong and crime,
  He walked the dark earth through.
The lust of power, the love of gain,
  The thousand lures of sin
Around him had no power to stain
  The purity within.

    *   *   *   *

Oh, Spirit of that early day !
  So pure and strong and true,
Be with us in the narrow way,
  Our faithful fathers knew.
Give strength the evil to forsake,
  The cross of Truth to bear,
And love and reverent fear to make
  Our lives a daily prayer !

                    John G. Whittier.

Early Friends in Newcastle and Gateshead.

"Shall we learn in our ease to forget,
To the martyrs of truth and of duty, our debt?"

THOUGH Carlyle tells us that "George's huge *Journal*, to
our regret, has no dates," but the "facts everywhere lie
around him like the leather parings of his old shop," we
know that George Fox's ministry commenced in 1647 in the
midlands; that in 1652 he "travelled on" through the
Yorkshire dales, to Firbank in Westmoreland, and on "the
top of a rock hard by the chapel" there he declared "God's
everlasting Truth and word of life" for "about the space
of three hours" to "above a thousand people." Many were
convinced, including "all the teachers of that congregation."
From the time of that journey Quakerism was established.
From that point and from Swarthmore it radiated.

Going thus back nearly two centuries-and-a-half, we
are in the days of Oliver Cromwell, Captain-General, and of
the Little Parliament, days before John Milton had "fallen
blind in the public service," when the population of England
and Wales was "perhaps five millions," and the National
Debt was "only £88,000." If we could look back we
should not know, says Macaulay, "one landscape in a
hundred." Nor could we trace much resemblance in the
religious condition of the people. For, in a petition to
Parliament about the date named, the Mayor of a northern
town, whose words are recorded in the King's Pamphlets,

B

wrote "we are a people who have been destitute of a preaching minister—yea, ever since any of us who are now breathing were born," and "ten or twelve parishes all adjoining are in like manner void of the means of salvation." Then there were fierce contentions as to dogma, wordy contests as to doctrine that "rent and tore the nation in spirit and principle from one end to the other."

Quakerism did not show itself in Newcastle until some years after Fox's first northern visit. And when it did it failed to gain "a local habitation." There was meeting-room given early in Sunderland and Shields. Newcastle refused it for forty years. It is difficult to say by whom the first attempt to propagate the new faith was made; but amongst the early preachers here were Thomas Taylor, Miles Halhead, John Audland, John Stubbs, John Camm, Francis Howgill, Richard Hubberthorne, George Fox, and George Whitehead. The difficulties they had to contend with were great, as for years their meetings were held in peril of imprisonment, and for their testimonies to the Truth, as they esteemed it, they had to suffer fines and spoilings of goods, committals to gaol, and sometimes incarceration until death. Two extracts will show how Quakers were treated and were esteemed nearly two centuries-and-a-half ago:—

"George Humble, of Sunderland, died at Durham, being a prisoner there for the testimony of Truth, and was buried in Durham burial ground in 1657."

"In 1654, Broughton Church declared that John Wilkinson, the pastor, departed to the Quakers, to his great shame and infamy. The Lord at last convince him of his sin. Amen. Amen. Amen."

The same volume quotes from Hexham Baptist Church Records a statement of the excommunication of several members—one "for joining the Quakers." *

The early Friends who visited Newcastle had to bear their share of contumely and imprisonment, though the records do not fully detail all the sufferings. Thus, early in

* Baptist Churches in the North of England.

1653, John Audland "was imprisoned at Newcastle-on-Tyne," and Miles Halhead was also committed, as we shall see. Thomas Taylor, who had been a clergyman at Richmond, and left the church because he had become convinced of Friends' views, says little of his visit to Tyneside. Writing to Margaret Fell Fox, he says that he tried to get a Hebrew Lexicon in Newcastle, "but the stationers had it not," and he got one later for 10/- from a person "related to me in the outward."

Miles Halhead, a husbandman, of Underbarrow, was one of Fox's early converts. He visited Newcastle, "where the Mayor and Sheriff committed him to prison, but very soon let him go, the Mayor being troubled with doubts as to whether they had done right in imprisoning him."

Again, in 1653, John Audland (born 1630, near Kendal), a preacher at Firbank, who had been convinced by George Fox, visited Newcastle, with John Stubbs, a Lancastrian schoolmaster and author. They were imprisoned here. Their visit was followed by the issue of five or six tracts written against the Quakers—three by Alderman Thomas Ledgerd, and another, "The Perfect Pharisee under Monkish Holiness," written by several clergymen. James Naylor and others wrote replies to these.*

The record of visits of George Fox himself may next be given from his quaint *Journal*.

About 1657, George Fox says that he came "to Newcastle, where I had once been before." With Anthony Pearson he visited "one Ledger, an alderman of the town," who had said that Friends "lived in the fells like butter-

---

* Two at least of these tracts are locally printed. One is "printed by S. B., Newcastle," and a second is "printed by S. B., Gateside." Naylor's tract is excluded from his collected works.

From 1656 to 1660 there were at least 34 tracts issued on behalf of Friends, now bound in one volume in Newcastle Library. The printers are generally "Thomas Simmons, at the Bull and Mouth," Giles Calvert, at the Black-spread Eagle ; and Robert Wilson, at the Black-spread Eagle and Windmill.

flies," but who would not yield to allow them to have a meeting. Ledger "began to plead for the Sabbath-day. I told him they kept markets and fairs on that which was the Sabbath-day." So in George Fox's words a little meeting had to be got "at the Gatesyde."

It will be noticed that Fox speaks of having visited Newcastle previously. An examination of the original copy of his *Journal* shows that no definite mention of the time of that previous visit is made; but it evidently was in 1653. Another comment may be made: Alderman "Ledger" compared Quakers to butterflies because of their living in the fells; but in one of the books written against Quakers by five Newcastle clergymen, a year or two before, the writers say "we find no place hears so much of their [Friends'] religion as streets and market crosses."

The Friend who accompanied George Fox on his visit to Alderman Ledgerd was Anthony Pearson, of Rampshaw Hall, near Auckland, a "Justice of the Peace in three counties," to whose house two visits were paid by George Fox. Anthony Pearson (born about 1628) is described in the State Papers as having been when 20 years old Clerk to "Sir Arthur Hasselrigg." A letter to Gerard Roberts, in 1659, says that "Gervase Benson and Anthony Pearson were put out for conscience sake" from the Commission of the Peace. In that year he was Clerk to a Friends' General Meeting in Durham. He wrote a valuable work on Tithes, from the Quaker standpoint. It is believed that he left the Society of Friends a little later. The State Papers furnish some facts in support of this belief, though in 1661 Sir P. Musgrave denounced him as a "Quaker" who corresponded with the disaffected party. Pearson was examined, and denied any such correspondence. He says, however, that in the old [Cromwellian] time he "embraced the chimerical notions of those times, and ran into excesses in zeal for religion." A letter in 1665 in the same State Papers describes "Anthony Pearson, the great Quaker, as undersherife" of Durham, and a record of his death quoted in Bishop Cosin's life leaves little doubt that he had ceased to be a Friend.

It is not known exactly who were Fox's companions, in addition to Anthony Pearson; but it is believed that they were Alexander Parker and Robert Widders. Both of these were the frequent associates of Fox in home and foreign travel. A local coincidence is worth noticing. Ledgerd was told by George Fox that they "kept markets and fairs on that which was the Sabbath-day." Very soon after this, the Newcastle ministers "moved the Council to petition the Lord Protector to change the market from Saturday to Friday," and the petition was sent.

George Whitehead, born at Orton, Westmorland, in 1635, became in 1652 one of Fox's followers, sharing in the evangelistic work, and in its penalties, and its imprisonments. Frequently he pleaded personally with Charles the Second for mercy and toleration; and he applied with more success to James the Second. He headed a deputation to William the Third on the tithe and oath question, and he joined in presenting an address to George the First.

George Whitehead says that he visited, in the former part of the winter of 1657, meetings northward to Newcastle and Northumberland. Accompanied by Richard Wilson, a Friend of Sunderland, he went to the "small meeting of Friends at Berwick," and then went to Holy Island, where the wife of the governor of the garrison or fort there was a Friend. They were kindly received in the Island, had a meeting there "in the Castle," and the governor, Captain Phillips, became "convinced of the truth." He and his wife removed into Oxfordshire, "to Banbury side, and so far as I know, both continued Friends to the end."

Whitehead continues, "our loving Friend, John Dove,* and his wife and family at Whittlesey kindly received me

* In the original Journal of George Fox it is stated that Lieut. Dove left the army because he had embraced Friends' views.

at his house." He then goes on to refer to attempts to hold
a meeting in Newcastle, and says—

"The Mayor of the town (influenced by the Priests), would
not suffer us to keep any meeting within the Liberty of the
Town, though in Gateside (being out of the Mayor's Liberty)
our Friends had settled a meeting, at our beloved Friend,
Richard Ubank's house. . . . The first meeting we then
endeavoured to have within the town of Newcastle was in a
large room taken on purpose by some Friends; William Coatesworth, of South Shields, with other friends, being zealously
concerned for the same. The meeting was not fully gathered
when the Mayor of the Town and his Officers came, and, by
force, turned us out of the meeting; and not only so, but out
of the Town also; for the Mayor and his Company commanded
us and went along with us as far as the Bridge over the river
Tine that parts Newcastle and Gateshead; upon which Bridge
there is a Blew Stone to which the Mayor's Liberty extends;
when we came to the stone, the Mayor gave his charge to
each of us in these Words, viz —' *I charge and command you in
the name of His Highness the Lord Protector. That you come
no more into Newcastle to have any more meetings there at your
peril.*'

On a first day later they met again in Newcastle out-
doors, but the Mayor's officers took them to the Bridge as
before. Some Friends tried to have a meeting in "The
Guildhall" (the old Moot Hall), and the keeper let it for
that purpose, but "a Priest of the Town, said to be ——
Hammond" interposed, and with a bribe of 2s. 6d. persuaded
the keeper to run from his bargain. An out-door meeting
was held, "on the side of the hill near the Shire House,"
and George Whitehead had there a splendid service, some
saying that he was heard "over the river Tyne into Gateshead."

The meeting at Richard Ubank's was probably the
meeting to which Gateshead Friends removed from Pipewellgate, where they first met, whilst the minister
"Hammond" was, of course, Samuel Hammond, a noted
Divine, who came to Newcastle from Bishop Wearmouth, being appointed by Newcastle Council "preacher at

Nicholas' Church." He left Newcastle about the time of the
Act of Uniformity in 1662, went to Hamburg and Stock-
holm, finally settling at Hackney, and dying there in 1666.
George Whitehead's account adds that William Coatesworth
proposed to go to London to lodge a complaint against the
authorities of Newcastle, but he did not carry out the
intention.

The visits of the early Friends were to a Newcastle
without railways, without gas, without great factories,
without public parks; a Newcastle comprised within the
walls, with trade ruled by Guilds; an era when coal was
taxed to rebuild London after the great fire, and to rebuild
fifty-two parish churches; and when in St. John's Church,
Westgate, Alderman Christopher Nicholson officiated at
marriages, as in the case of Ambrose Barnes. It was to
Newcastle after the infliction of the plague. and the possession by the Scots; to Newcastle when baronets lived in
the Close; and to Newcastle when the old Tyne Bridge
was narrow and "crowded with houses which clustered
upon its battlements." And the district was widely
different, for industry was in infancy towns of to-day
were undreamt of, rivers were shallow streams, and travel
was chiefly on horseback or by foot on poor roads.

Finding, then, no foothold in Newcastle, the Friends
met in Gateshead, in Pipewellgate, in what was afterwards,
and is now, the Fountain tavern. Before the end of 1660
they became tenants of a house in High Street, Gateshead
(on the site of which, in 1731, the Powell's almshouses were
built), for in Whitehead's memoirs he speaks of Friends,
before 1660, meeting at Richard Ewbank's, as we have
seen. Up to 1698 Friends met in Gateshead, held their
meetings for worship and for church affairs there; buried
there their dead, and endured something of the storm of
persecution that fell upon the Quakers throughout the
land. From denominational records and from local histories
examples of these sufferings may be given :—

In 1656, the Newcastle Merchant Adventurers decided that "no Popish recusant, Quaker," or any one who did not attend the public ordinances, should be taken apprentice.

In 1660, a prisoner in Durham gaol says in a letter to a London Friend that there were "Ninety and odd in Prison," most committed for refusing to take oath. The prisoners would not pay the gaoler 2s. 6d. per week each for their beds, so he "threw twenty of us into a Stinking Dungeon where we could not all lie down at once." The High Sheriff was more merciful, and had them removed to the House of Correction.

In 1661, some 27 persons were taken from a meeting at Robert Linton's, at South Shields, by the Deputy Governor of "Tinmouth Castle," "and cast into nasty Holes there, where they lay a full Month," and were then cast out,—without apparent authority for apprehension or dismission. The list of Friends so treated includes John Blakling, of Sedburg; John Dove and William Dove, of Whitley, yeomen; Mary Dove, jun., spinster; George Linton, Robert Linton, of South Shields; and William Maud, of Sunderland.

In 1678, Patrick Livingstone, who was preaching in Gateshead meeting, was violently struck, and afterwards sent to prison.

In 1681, six local members of the Society of Friends were fined for meeting for worship, and goods destrained to the value of £55.

In 1684, John Hedley, servant to a Friend named Christopher Bickers, of Gateshead, was cruelly whipped for declining to aid in the distraint on his master's goods.

A petition to the king for relief to Friends in 1684 states that 39 "Durham Friends" were in prison.

In 1684, Gateshead parish book has an entry of payment "for carrying 26 Quakers to Durham £2 17s. 0d." Our records say that in that year Justices Jenkins and Isaac Basire came into Gateshead meeting, caused the Friends to be taken to an inn, tendered the oath to

J. Tisick and John Allot, of Newcastle, and John Airey
and Math. Allason, of Gateshead, and on their refusal to
swear they were sent to " Durham Jaile, and kept three
weeks." Later in the same year five men and three women
were sent to the house of correction for eleven weeks for
refusing to swear.

In 1686, the Under Sheriff of the County of Durham
made a return of the Quakers or persons reputed Quakers in
the County of Durham convicted as recusants.

There were 323 in all, including 17 at Gateshead,
4 at Jarrow, 2 at Monkton, 1 at Heworth, and 1 at
Whickham. At Gateshead there were Christopher Bickers
and his wife; John Doubleday, Lionel Hetherington
(sadler); Moses ffisher and his wife; John Ayre the
elder; John Ayre the younger; Wm. ffenwick and his
wife; John Allinson and his wife; Matthew Allenson
and his wife; Robert Mooney and his wife; and Barbara
Hunter.

Friends were kept out of the local governing bodies ;—
even an Act of Parliament* reciting the provisions for
re-electing church trustees at Newcastle excludes them
specifically,—the person to be chosen " not being one of
the people called Quakers." They could not be buried
usually in churchyards, and hence pitiful records in local
registers such as this:—" A child of Henry Grainger, a
Quaker, buried in his garden," or " Thomas Arey," master
and mariner, " buried in Jo. Dove's burying place " at
Cullercoats.

A burial ground was attached to the meeting-house at
Gateshead, in which it is stated that about one hundred
interments took place. From 1669 down to about 1724,
there are burials at Gateshead. In several cases, there
were interments of Tyneside Friends in the gardens of
their relatives. In the list of burials of Friends is that of
Abigail Tizacke. The inscription on the tombstone now

*All Saints Rebuilding Act, 1786.

near the carriage drive in the Armstrong Park, Newcastle, is :—

ABIGALL TIZACKE
DAUGHTER OF JOHN & SARAH TIZACKE
DEPTD THIS LIFE
YE 7TH DAY OF YE 12TH MONTH,
AND IN YE 7TH WEACK OF HER AGE.
ANNO 1679.

Diligent enquiry fails to trace the cause of the transfer of this tombstone to the Park :—whether from Gateshead burial ground, or from the father's garden at the Glasshouses.

"The Register Book of the Burials of the People of God in scorn called Quakers, and others their relations and kindred who have been buried in their burying ground in Gateshead in the County of Durham." This is the quaint title of the record of the burials at Gateshead. There are cases of interment also in gardens, as at the Glasshouses, Newcastle, where Benjamin Tyttory (son of Daniel Tyttory, broad glass maker) was interred.

From the commencement of the Society on Tyneside a number of Friends resided in Newcastle, and some also at Gateshead and Jarrow. A desire was long felt to obtain a meeting house in Newcastle. About 1688, a site was sought in "Denton Chaire"—then one of the main thoroughfares,—but the project fell through. As the lease of the Gateshead meeting house neared its close, a later effort resulted in 1697 in the purchase of a site in Pilgrim Street, for £120. The deeds for the land are still extant, going back to 1600. The conveyance in December, 1697, was to John Doubleday, William Mitford, and Jeremiah Hunter, as trustees for the Society of Friends. The building of a Meeting House was commenced early in 1698, in what was then a rural locality, though in a main thoroughfare. A burial ground occupied part of the site purchased ; and in it, before the completion of the meeting house, the first interment took place—that of Philip Simpson, a labourer, on the 15th of 5th month, 1698. The last burial in this graveyard was that of George Richardson, in August, 1862.

The change from Gateshead to Newcastle may be further shown from the records of the Society. At the Monthly Meeting, 18th of 10th month, 1697, a minute states that " Its agreed att this Meeting yt a request be made to the next Quarterly Meeting for assistance towards building a meeting house in ye Town of Newcastle, and yt Joshua Middleton, Wm. Midford, John Fayrer" and other Friends are " to lay it before the Quarterly Meeting."

This was evidently done, and the minutes of the Quarterly Meeting record, on the 28th of 4th month, 1698, that the following subscriptions had been received from meetings at the places named :—

					£	s	d
Sunderland	...	...	...	...	£11	12	0
Stockton	...	...	...	...	10	16	6
Darlington	.	...	...	...	8	16	6
Raby	...	...	...	...	5	7	6
Auckland	...	...	...	...	5	12	6
Durham	...	...	...	...	8	3	6
Yarm	...	...	...	...	1	15	0
Barnard Castle		...	...	...	1	5	0
					£53	8	6

This considerable sum was thus raised by eight meetings Three other meetings desired to be excused from contributing : Shields, because it " had lately built a meeting house ; " Shotton, because it was about to rebuild one " at its own proper charge ; " and " Derwentwater " because the Friends there had lately built one at " their own charge."

On the 14th of 9th month, 1698, the meeting house at Newcastle must have been finished, for on that date Gateshead Monthly Meeting decided that the weekly meetings [for worship] should be held in the Pilgrim Street meeting house. In November, 1698, the last Monthly Meeting [for church business] was held in

Gateshead; and a little later, these meetings were begun
in Newcastle. Finally, at the Monthly Meeting at Sunderland on 13th November, 1699, Newcastle Friends
informed the meeting they had thought "fitt to Discontinue
Goatshead meeting house." There were evidently interments
for some time later in the burial-ground at Gateshead; but
there is the ultimate statement that the meeting house,
Gateshead, the messuage, garden, yard, etc., formerly
belonging to Richard Ewbank, tailor, deceased, and hereto-
fore in the possession of John Doubleday, his under-
tenants and assigns, was purchased in 1730 by trustees
under Thomas Powell's will for almshouses. In 1750, the
wife and grand-daughter of Stephenson (who had been
the surviving trustee) conveyed it to the churchwardens
and overseers of Gateshead. The situation is described as
"between the Goat on the top of the steep hill and the
Tolbooth or Popish Chapel." There are now three almshouses, built at different times, and extending from High
Street (opposite Swinburne Street) to the full length of
Powell's Court.

It may be added that the Gateshead meeting house had
been registered at Durham in the first year of William
and Mary for the use of "the People of God called
Quakers"; and other meetings then registered included
one held at "Robert Linton's house," South Shields; one
at Sunderland, at Robert Wardell's, and another held at
the "new building" in Bishop Wearmouth parish. Some
of the original forms of registration are still preserved.

Gateshead meeting, with those of Shields and Sunderland, were grouped as a monthly meeting. The name
given to it was "Goatshead Monthly Meeting," and it
had been almost invariably held at Gateshead. But in
1698 the meeting decided—"For ye sake of some antient
Friends of Sunderland and Shields that request it, who
through Infirmity of body cannot attend it here"—that
the meeting should be "kept in a course for some time,

and so to be at Shields next," then at Sunderland, then at Newcastle, and so on by turns.

A change was made in the name of the meeting. The minutes of the following monthly meeting held at Shields in the 11th month, 1698, begin—" Att the monthly meeting of Goateshead, Shields, and Sunderland Friends," and the meeting adjourned to Newcastle. A month or two later the heading is—" Att our monthly meeting of Newcastle, Shields, and Sunderland Friends," and finally it becomes for many years " att our monthly meeting."

The story of the attempts to hold a meeting of the Society of Friends in Newcastle thus extends over more than forty-four years. There is no known record of the numbers of the Quakers who met in the early days of the body at Gateshead and at Newcastle, nor are there other than scanty records of leading Friends. But there are many references to the Doubledays, the Middletons, the Aireys, and to Jeremiah Hunter, and Archibald Gillespie, of some of whom a few facts are ascertainable.

Robert Doubleday, of Jarrow, had two sons, John and Humphrey. John, born about 1661, who had advanced money to the owner of Alnwick Abbey, became its purchaser. He died December 15th, 1751, aged 90 years, leaving two sons. Michael Doubleday, one of these, is the " somewhat eccentric " Quaker whom the historian of Alnwick tells us went to see the Duke of Northumberland on business, wearing his hat. A servant removed the head gear and forgot to restore it till the Duke said—" Run with it and place it on his head or it may be the dearest that ever entered the castle." Michael Doubleday died unmarried at Alnwick Abbey, February, 1797, aged 73 years, and his landed estate at Alnwick was sold to the Duke of Northumberland.

John Doubleday, of Alnwick Abbey, is recorded in the Ellison (Jarrow) pedigree, as marrying Anne (Coan),

widow of George Ellison, of Hebburn, *after* 1683. In
1708, he signed, with thirteen other Friends, the address
to Queen Anne congratulating her on her escape from
" the Mischievous and Wicked Designs of her Enemies."

John Doubleday, jun.. married the daughter of " Robert
Barclay, sen., of *Wice*," and grand-daughter of the
famous Robert Barclay of the same place (Urie). A
Friends' meeting was held at Alnwick Abbey,* where
Thomas Storey, in 1728, stopped on a brief visit to John
Doubleday, jun. The second son of Robert Doubleday, of
Jarrow, Humphrey, was ancestor to George (partner in
Doubleday and Easterby), and to Thomas Doubleday,
politician, poet, and essayist.

A " *Testimony concerning Jeremiah Hunter* " was issued
by Durham Quarterly Meeting, which states that he was
born at Benfieldside in 1658; came to Newcastle as an
apprentice. and continued there as a fitter. About 25 years
of age he appeared " in public testimony for Truth." He
died 24/12/1741, aged 83 years,—having been a minister
about 58 years. Jeremiah Hunter left the value of a house
in Pandon, £80, " to encourage industrious poor Friends, as
Friends might see a service, that the truly deserving might
have the benefit."

John Doubleday and Jeremiah Hunter were two of
the trustees of Newcastle Meeting House. The third was
William Midford or Mitford. He is believed to have been
a master mariner. He died in 1737; and one of his latest
public efforts is referred to in the records of the Merchant
Company's Court at Newcastle, which state that in 1733 a
letter from him was " redd " setting forth the hardships
sustained by reason of the penalty on any one taking a
Quaker as apprentice and asking for the repeal of the Act.

* Alnwick Abbey meeting was kept up to the middle of the eighteenth
century. A Newcastle Friend still possesses a pamphlet, '' A Call to
Repentance," which an owner of old had endorsed—" This book was sent
me from a meeting of Quakers at Alnwick Abbey, 1746."

HANNAH MIDDLETON GURNEY.

Probably the best known of the early Newcastle Quakers were members of the Middleton family. Joshua Middleton (son of John Middleton, draper), of Darlington, was born there in 1647. He associated himself with Friends in that town, and was more than once convicted for attending Quaker meetings at the houses of Friends such as Robert Truman and Cuthbert Thompson. In one summons he is described as "Joshua Middleton, mercer." In Surtees's History of Durham a list of freeholders in Darlington is given, in which are two entries as under :—

"Joshua Middleton (Quaker)."

"Edward Fisher (Quaker)."

Not very long after this date Joshua Middleton removed to Newcastle, and for many years he and his family were amongst the chief workers in Tyneside Quakerism. His son Joshua married one of the Doubledays; his daughter Hannah (sometimes spoken of as " the fair Quaker") was married to Joseph Gurney, of Norwich. Daniel Gurney's book on " The House of Gournay" gives a portrait of Hannah Middleton Gurney, a "comely woman, with a nice face" says one of her descendants. Hannah Middleton Gurney's great-granddaughter, Emma Gurney, married in 1825 Joseph Pease, of Southend, Darlington, the "first Quaker member of the House of Commons." And these descendants of the Middletons share largely in Durham rule. In 1702 Joshua Middleton was one of the Friends who signed (and probably presented) the address from the yearly meeting to the Queen. Thomas Storey records several visits to Newcastle, staying in 1717 twice at Joshua Middleton's house. In 1725, he lodged at the "widow Jean Middleton's house," where he was a guest on other visits. Joshua Middleton died in 11th month, 1720 ; and his widow in 1738.

To John Airey, of Newcastle, it is believed that one of the letters recording the death of George Fox was sent. This "John Airey, soap-boiler, in Newcastle," is recorded in

C

"Letters of Early Friends" as the country correspondent of the first Meeting for Sufferings [1675] for both Durham and Northumberland.

John Airey, sen., died in 1693, the interment being at Gateshead in that year. His wife, Rebeckah Airey, was also interred at Gateshead, 24th of 8th month, 1705. Their son, John, is referred to in Newcastle Merchant Adventurers' Records, when in 1739, it is reported, that "John Airey, a Quaker, kept shop, and retailed grocerys," though he was not a freeman. He was interviewed, but with little result. Financial trouble came to the Airey family, and later records are slight.

Newcastle *Monthly* Meeting issued a testimony concerning *Archibald Gillespy*, who died at Newcastle, 30/10/1755, aged nearly 89 years, having been a minister 62 years, and who was buried in the Friends' burial ground, Newcastle.

Archibald Gillespie and Anthony Watson were desired in 1703 to provide a room in Hexham against the next Quarterly Meeting. (Allendale Monthly Meeting Records). A. G. lived long in Allendale.

About 1701, Samuel Bownas (who was originally a blacksmith) says that he sometimes stayed at Gateshead at "honest William Simpson's; I did occasionally help them in their business, he being a blacksmith." This little fact shows how the early Quaker ministers had at times to support themselves. Samuel Bownas's later career in London and in America is well known.

The Tyzack and Tytory families were amongst those who early became Friends in Newcastle. They left Loraine through the persecution of Protestants there, and settled in Tyneside at the Glasshouses. A lease for ground, "including the Glasshouses . . . . . . boundering on Ouseburn on the west," was granted by Newcastle Council, in 1638, to Sir R. Mansell, who employed many of these religious refugees. Amongst those who became

Friends were Daniel Tytory; Paul Tyzack, and Jane, his
wife; Peregrine Tyzack, and John and Sarah Tyzack
(parents of the little girl whose tombstone is in the
Armstrong Park, Newcastle). In 1684 John Tyzack was
imprisoned for refusing to swear. In 1684 he removed to
London, where "bonds and afflictions" awaited him, for he
was one of those tried at the Guildhall for holding a
Quakers' meeting near to Angel Court. The Glasshouses,
at Newcastle, continued for many years to be a residence for
glass-making Quakers. Newcastle Corporation records show
that in the year 1684 a lease of one of the glasshouses was
given to John Henzell, Peregrine Tyzack, and partners.
And, in 1698, Joshua Middleton is "mentioned as the owner
of a glasshouse in Newcastle." Middleton was connected
with the Tyzacks by marriage.

The Certificate of removal for John and Sarah Tyzack,
issued by the Monthly Meeting at Goateshead, the 13th of
y^d 12th month, 1687/8, is as follows:—

> "To all Friends whom it may consern in London
> Whereas John Tizack late of the Town and County of
> Newcastle upon Tyne, Broad Glassmaker, being desirous of
> a Certificate from our Monthly Meeting for himself and his
> wife we have thought fit to certifie as follows, viz. :
>
> "That our friend John Tizack, aforesd. did for many
> years owne and make profesion of the pretious Truth with
> us, and was of good Report even until the time that he was
> called to remove himselfe and family to London to settle
> there. He was very dilligent in frequenting Meetings as
> often as his calling would permit. He had his share in
> sufferings, both in being knocked at the meeting and
> imprisonment. He was very dilligent in his calling and
> was ready to contribute with us to such as stood in need or
> otherwise as we had occasion.—— And as for Sarah his
> wife she was of good Report amongst us, esteemed a sober
> discreet woman, loved Truth and ffriends, frequented
> meetings, and was a good Savour where she dwelt. They
> removed from hence to London in the year 1684.
>
> "So in Love and ffeare of God on whom wee have
> believed wee dearly Salute you and remain
>
> Yo^r ffriends
>
> John Ayrey   George Tizack   Jane Turner

Robt. Linton	Jas. Harrison	Dorothy Smith
Chr. Bickers	Thos. Wilkinson	Annie Hunter
Tho. Chandler	Moses fficher	Joane Lynton
John Allott	Lyonl. Heather-	Mary Softley
Robt. Wallis	ington	Sarah Wallis
John Morton	Geo. Raw	Elizabeth Hazoll
John Greete	Wm. Appleby	Anne Muschamp
Jer. Hunter	Robt. Softley	Sarah Hunter
Wm. Smith	———— ————	Anne Corneath
Danll. Fittery	Rebecca Ayrey	Margaret Simpson
Samll. ffreeman	Barbara Midford	Catherine Elliott
Robt. Askew	Jane ffearon	Elizabeth fficher "

Of the Friends who thus signed the certificate John Airey and John Allott had suffered imprisonment at the same time as John Tyzack.

The Kings were a local and numerous Quaker family. The birth of James King is recorded in 1668, and down to 1790, there were 83 Kings born in Newcastle meeting— some of the parents being weavers, grocers, glassmakers, mariners, coopers, and agents. There is not much to be said as to the places of residence of the early Friends. Benjamin Atkinson, tailor, lived at the " foot of the Long Stairs, Close," Edward King, weaver, lived in 1670 at " The Burn ;" John Allott, a keelman, lived in historic Sandgate ; John and Ann Doubleday, at Jarrow ; and Jeremiah Hunter probably in Pandon. Two or three Friends lived near the Castle Garth, and many as we have seen, at the Glasshouses ; whilst Gateshead had for some time a number.

This, then, is the story of the Society of Friends in its early days at Gateshead and Newcastle. It outlived in its first century the fiercest blasts of the storm of persecution. These years take us through the Protectorate, and through the reigns of Charles, James, William and Mary, Anne, and down to the end of that of George II. Gradually the Society was consolidated. It held its meetings undisturbed by mayor or constable ; it began to build up its mode of church government ; it took steps to make its simple method of marriage clear and public. It ascertained in the constituent meetings the " clearness from other marriage engagements" of those about to be married. It answered " Queeries" intended to bring to the greater gatherings the state of the local societies ; it appointed overseers to " warn the unruly," and to minister to the needy ; and it endeavoured to fulfil the best functions of a Church.

As the years go by, the first generation of Friends pass away—the names of Joshua and Jean Middleton, of Jeremiah Hunter, John and Katherine Fayrer, Robert and Ann Doubleday, and Reginald Holme cease to appear in the minute books. A second generation such as Samuel and Joseph King, Thomas Hodgson, William Little, John Freeman, and Jonathan Raine " have their day and cease to be." Then from Whitby came John Richardson to wed Margaret Stead, and become the head of a vast family ; from London Jonathan Ormston came ; from near Settle the Claphams ; from Allendale the Watsons ; and others whose names are still represented on the member-roll of the Society.

The
Premises in Pilgrim Street.

(Contributed by Thomas Pumphrey.)

THIS Chapter can have but little interest for any but local Friends; but as the history of the premises extends over two hundred years, it is fitting that some account of their purchase, and adaptation, from time to time, to the varying needs of the Congregation, should find a place in the history of the people who have occupied them.

The accompanying plans have been reduced from existing plans with the help of the Deeds and other descriptive documents where such were available, but the exact lines of the original buildings can only be regarded as approximate, inasmuch as tradition has been called to supplement the fragmentary data at command. Numbers 1 and 2 must therefore be taken *cum grano salis*.

The site is well defined. It presented the same frontage as at present to Pilgrim Street; it seems clear that the cottage adjoining the entrance was used as a Caretaker's dwellinghouse; that there was an open yard between this and the Meeting House; and that the original House was probably on much the same lines as its successor, but perhaps not so lofty, and more dimly lighted.

The ground behind or to the east of the Meeting House reached down to the "Airick" or Erick Burn, and was used as a grave-yard from the first year of occupation (1698, 5th month, 15th,) but the records do not state whether any of the earlier interments took place in this

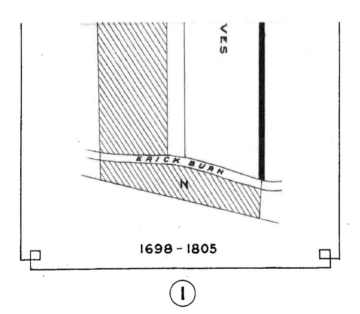

1698 - 1805

1

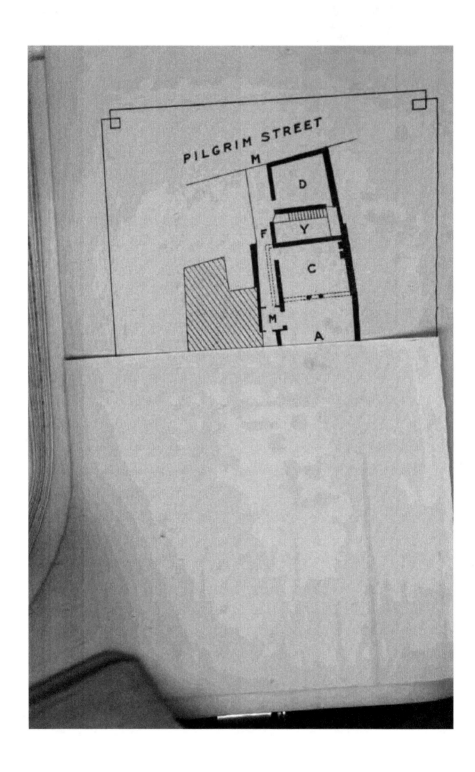

ground—presumably in Gateshead. A separate chapter will give further facts relative to burials.

In 1805 the original House and Caretaker's cottage were re-built.

The back part or western end was covered by a gallery or " loft " with several tiers of raised seats, access to which was by an open staircase from the entrance lobby, and across the cottage yard by an over-head gangway.

Underneath this " loft " was appropriated to the purposes of the Women's Meetings for Discipline, and was divided at such times from the main part of the Meeting House by removable shutters.

The access both to the Meeting House and grave-yard was by a long narrow passage, the lower part, below the porch-entrance to the Meeting House proper, was open to the sky and sloped steeply down to the grave-yard level. The porch is described as a little to the east of the present door.

In 1813 additional accommodation was obtained by lengthening the Meeting House at both ends.

A letter has just come to light written by Hadwen Bragg, to his friends George Richardson and Daniel Oliver, in which he describes in detail how after the alterations at the eastern end had been carried out he had apparently with difficulty, pursuaded his cautious friend, David Sutton, to consent to the further change at the other end of the building ; but he had better describe it in his own words :—

"Hadwen Bragg to George Richardson and Daniel Oliver,
Travelling on Religious Service.

Summerhill, 8th Mo. 26th, 1813.

Dear Friends,

George and Daniel,

It feels pleasant to assure you of our often remembering you with near affection and best wishes ; the information hitherto received of your movements has been very acceptable, though I have been fearful of your using too great exertion for your bodily health and strength. . . . It will be pleasant to you to know that the proposed extension of our Meeting House was accomplished, and that it appears very agreeable to all. I am told that Robert Omston had expressed

much pleasure on seeing its airyness and enlargement, he and
Catherine returned about a week since, but from my being
at Shields on 1st day I have not yet seen them. When all
was finished about the Men's end of the house, we soon
prevailed upon dear David Sutton to agree to the extension
of the Women's, which is now nearly finished, and will afford
space for three rows of seats of two each being added. I hope
this when completed will also be to general satisfaction and
prove of real utility ; perhaps an encroachment upon the Cloak
closet is the only doubtful point ; but this I hope will not be
serious, though my dear M. B. feels keenly fearful of its
unfavourable consequences. The extension of 6ft. 8ins. will
exhibit a level ceiling with that part which before was level,
quite through I think to neighbour Coulson's wall, that is,
there is no break under the stairs to the Gallery. Covering the
roof with lead upon plank, enables us to have it more flat and
extending to C. Jackson's wall. We let the water from the other
roof and it descends by the roof over the lobby back to the spout
which already takes off a part into the conduit outside the east
end of the lobby. The parapet wall which will be formed in
front with a 3 inch coping, from the front of the Cloak closet to
C. Jackson's wall, we expect will look pretty well. The
entrance of the Lobby is proposed to be without doors, letting
the present ones remain where they are ; the two windows are
placed a little nearer the lobby and a four foot square skylight
is a little north of the middle of the new roof. I think it is
doubtful whether we shall have so much light as could be
desired, but there will be most near the clerks' seat. Two iron
columns of 5 inches diameter will be an ample support to an
excellent piece of foreign timber placed across. . . . .

The next change was in 1829, when the long strip of
ground was purchased on the south side of the grave-yard
footpath, and extending from the boundary of the adjoining
properties in Pilgrim Street down to the said Erick Burn.

At the western or higher end of this plot stood a house
which was included in the purchase, and this was apportioned
to the caretaker, as now ; the sum of £347 having been
expended upon the new property and in adapting the
vacated house in the front to the requirements of business
premises. An incidental gain to the comfort of the
congregation was the additional Lobby space afforded by
the approach to the new rooms.

Plan No. 4 also shews the addition of a piece of waste
ground through which the Burn ran at the east end of the
grave-yard, and the buildings which were erected in 1833,
for the accommodation of the First-day Schools which were
commenced in the following year. The small plot of

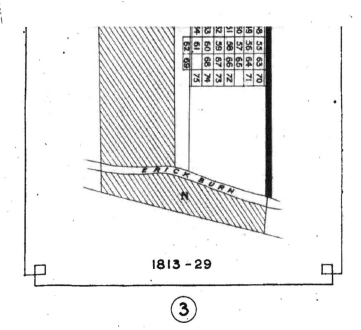

1813 - 29

③

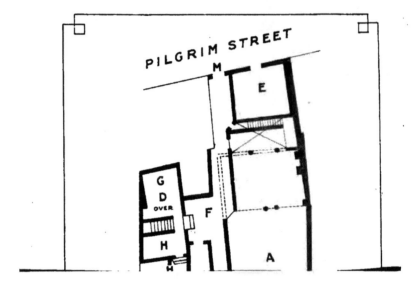

ground was granted free by the Corporation to straighten the boundary of the Street then being formed.

This important alteration is fully described in the following report of the Building Committee in the handwriting of George Richardson, and signed by William Holmes, who was the honorary Architect for the new extension.

"To the Preparative Meeting.

The Friends appointed as a Building Committee have endeavoured to carry into effect the various resolutions of the Meeting as expressed by its Minutes. The Title deed of the Ground granted by the Corporation has been duly executed and is enrolled agreeably to act of Parliament. The Building at the foot of the Burial ground and over the Carrier's Warehouse, &c , is now compleated and is nearly ready for occupation. A portion of it has been let to Richard Grainger, on Lease of 21 years, bearing rent from the 11th Mo. last, at Forty pounds pr. annum, including the annual consideration for the liberty of lights; Chantler & Co. are also to pay an addition of Ten pounds pr. annum for their improved accomadation. The whole rental of the property let is now One Hundred and Seventy pounds pr. annum. The new Dwellinghouse and Schoolroom are yet to let, though a person is in treaty as a tenant. The large room is nearly ready for the accomadation of Meetings for Discipline.

The alterations in the old Women's Meeting house are made, by the removal of the Shutters, which have been used in the new building; the door has been removed to the South west corner (which, in addition to other advantages, has enlarged the lobby), the apartment has been new painted and coloured, and on the whole is rendered more comfortable, and is a useful extension of accomadation for Meetings for worship. A door has also been placed at the foot of the stone stairs, which will tend to exclude the noise from the street, when the windows of the house are open for ventilation.

The attention of the Committee having been turned to the consideration of the best and most economical mode of providing the necessary addition of seats, which the new arrangements will require, concluded on the improvement of the construction of the old ones (of which we have so large a number) by the insertion of a middle rail, which with some other alterations, has rendered them much more comfortable. By the adoption of this plan, such new seats as are needful may be constructed after the same model, and thus the uniformity will be preserved, and every useful purpose answered. About ten new seats are in course of preparation (part of which are of old materials), and four are to be made without backs, to be introduced when the house is crowded.

Annexed is an Abstract of the Accounts for the year.

Signed on behalf of the Committee,

Newcastle,   WILLIAM HOLMES.
1st Mo., 25th, 1833.

Abstract of the Receipts and Disbursements of the Committee of management for the Property belonging to the Society of Friends of Newcastle, in Pilgrim Street, &c., from 1st Mo., 2nd, 1832, to 1st Mo., 21st, 1833, inclusive.

RECEIPTS.	£	s.	d.	DISBURSEMENTS.	£	s.	d.
Balance brought forward	41	0	3	Lodged with Backhouse & Co. ...	40	0	0
Rents of Property let	120	0	0	Interest paid to E. Cutforth... ...	8	0	0
Of Backhouse & Co. being Principal & Int. of lodgment	259	18	6	Do. Robt. Ormston, 3 payments ... Do. Wm Holmes ...	30 8	0 13	0 4
Money borrowed ...	960	0	0	Ground Rent to J. Morton	2	15	6
Due to Treasurer...	30	3	11	Repairs, &c.	3	10	6
				Gaol cess ... 2 15 10			
				Stamps ... 0 4 2			
					3	0	0
				Insurance of New Property	1	7	6
				Stabling for Carrier	2	0	0
				Jos. Watson, for Enrolment of Title	4	17	0
				New building and Improvments ...1261 10 9			
	1411	2	8	*Deduct* Materials			
Less Error ...	50	0	0	Sold ... 4 11 11			
					1256	18	10
	£1361	2	8		£1361	2	8

Total cost of the New Building and other improvements up to 1st Mo., 21st., 1833, inclusive:

			£	s.	d.
Mason work, labour and cartage ...	...	...	299	19	0
Joiner Work	...	...	191	16	1
Commission on labour	...	...	49	2	0
Timber	...	...	305	0	10½
Stones, Bricks, Plaster, &c.	...		107	11	0
Slater work	...	...	73	10	0
Plumber do.	...	...	77	0	0
Painting, Glazing, &c.	...	...	85	0	0
Hardware and Sundries	...	...	38	11	3
Smith work	...	...	29	8	8
			£1256	18	10½

Total amount of money borrowed, viz. :

			£	s.	d.
Of Robt. Ormston	...	...	500	0	0
Backhouse & Co.	..	...	300	0	0
Eliz. Cutforth	...	...	200	0	0
Wm. Holmes	...	...	350	0	0
Jon. Pristman & W. Bennet	300	0	0
Matt. Robson	...	...	110	0	0
			£1760	0	0

All at 4 pr. Cent Interest.

"In the above statement is comprised the New building, composed of a Dwellinghouse with Schoolroom. The large Room for Meetings of Discipline—the Stable rebuilt—the Carriers warehouse greatly improved by the lowering of the floor, fixing the Crane, &c. The convenience for Men Friends—the Women's yard with its appurtenances - the removal of the old buildings—levelling the ground—preparing a portion for burial-ground—the removal of the shutters of the Women's Meeting House—changing the door— enlarging the lobby—improving the outer passage—painting and colouring the part under the loft, &c.. &c., &c., also Glazing for the year."

The room described as a Men's Meeting House was that portion of the first floor facing into the grave-yard and divided from the long School-room by sliding wooden shutters. This room served the purpose for Preparative, Monthly and Quarterly Meetings for Men Friends until 1868, when the Women's House and the A Classrooms were built.

The School-room extended along the whole of the Manors frontage with access staircase at the North end; the girls classes met at that end and the boys in the portion abutting upon the said shutters.

The premises underneath were let off, partly as a warehouse, and partly (as appears from the Report just quoted) as a dwellinghouse, consisting of the ground floor and basement rooms.

Other rooms were let off to Richard Grainger, and were approached from the Arcade. These were on a different level from that of the School-room and Men's Meeting House.

In these new rooms the "Sabbath School" was commenced in 1834, as elsewhere more fully described, and about twenty years later "the Senior Class" was collected, at first in the Men's Meeting House, which gradually developed into the Adult School. This new departure was allocated to the basement storey of the Manors building, under the Infant Class-room.

These unfavourable conditions continued until 1867, when an appeal was made to Friends, and warmly responded to, for a further extension of premises in which the Adult School would have better scope for development, and a room provided more suitable for the Men's Meetings for Discipline.

The vacant ground, unused for burials, was therefore built upon, and the rooms now known as the Women's Meeting House and the A Class-rooms were built, the cellar under the latter being added to the large timber warehouse. The Meeting House lobby was levelled, considerably enlarged and reroofed, the warming system remodelled, the boiler being removed from under the large Meeting House. Considerable new plumbing work was done with some additional drainage, and the Meeting House furniture was mostly renewed.

In 1877 some internal alterations were effected in the Meeting House which added to its cheerfulness.

The western extension, made sixty-four years before, was added to the front shop together with the space occupied by the stairs to the "loft" which was removed ; the back wall was re-instated ; the floor raised in tiers ; the Ministers' gallery at the opposite end reduced in level and the panelled screen in front of it substituted by an open rail.

During these years the Adult School and Mission work were growing under the fostering hand of Frederick Clark and his colleagues. This called for an enlargement of the room where the Meetings of the latter were held. This was done by removing the partition from the centre of the A Class room.

The entrance from the Manors by the covered way was also greatly improved, substituting open iron gates for the old warehouse-like wooden ones, renewing the steps, and in other ways making it more inviting as an entrance to the premises.

A covered porch was also provided at the high end of the grave-yard and other minor improvements affected.

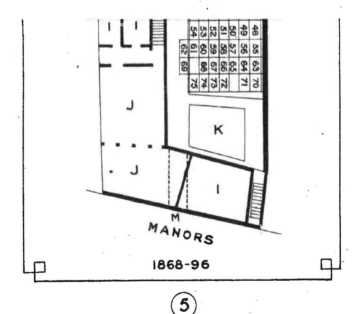

MANORS

1868-96

5

Provision was also made for kitchen and scullery operations
as an essential to the economical working of the numerous
teas and other social functions which have increased as
residential areas have widened. The following report of
the Property Committee will further explain other work
which was undertaken at the same time :—

"To the Preparative Meeting.

The Property Committee present the following Report
respecting the work that has been done on these premises in
connection with the Schools alterations.

The work was commenced in August, 1897, and the last of
the accounts was not presented until well into the following-
year.

Though a careful attempt has been made to classify the
charges under the separate heads of Current Account, and
Special Account, it has been found impracticable to do more
than approximate

	£	s.	d.
As the Account stands the 'Special' Schools alteration Account gives a total of ...	711	7	8
Towards which the sum of ... ... has been generously subscribed	542	15	0
Leaving a balance of	£168	12	8
to be added to the total Current account ...	557	13	10
	£726	6	6

This has been reduced by surplus balances of £189 on
Current account to £537.

The work not originally contracted for includes the
following. in addition to numerous smaller items which were
found necessary as the work proceeded, viz. :

A New Infant's Classroom and enlarging the old one.

Adapting the basement to the purposes of a heating
chamber ; protecting the room above from heat, etc.

Diverting and trapping the main drain and forming new
branch

Remodelling the roof of the offices formerly let to the
Grainger Estate.

Thoroughly repairing. the roofs of the Meeting House
Lobby ; providing snow gutters throughout for protection of
the slates ; Renewing the skylights to the Cloakroom and
making new window therein.

Overhauling the gas supply ; laying new and larger main
branches.

Fitting cooking and scullery apparatus in the B Classroom,
with sink, feed and waste.

Papering and painting the lower section of the premises throughout.

Reglazing all the side windows of the Women's Meeting House and A Classroom, and providing inner windows to the former.

Protecting the lower windows and glass screen-door with wire-guards.

Your Committee have done all this knowing that it would involve a considerable over-draft of their account. They have considered each item of large expenditure carefully in conference before sanctioning it, and have endeavoured to act in the interests of the Congregation, regarding it as their primary duty to adapt the premises to the requirements of Friends and the work they have in hand, and to do it as well as it could be done consistently with simplicity.

Had they not known that the annual balance on Current Account would suffice to gradually but certainly cancel the over-draft, they would not have felt warranted in undertaking the work; but they trust that in the long run the course they have adopted will be justified and approved.

The income from rents has been somewhat diminished by taking back from the Grainger Estate the rooms which were let to it, but there ought to be a yearly margin for maintenance of about £135; and as repairs ought not to be heavy for some years to come, your Committee think there is no need for any anxiety as to the deficit of £537 which at present stands against them at the Bank.

Signed,   JOHN W. PEASE,
EDWARD WATSON,
J. ALARIC RICHARDSON,
THOMAS PUMPHREY.

Newcastle, Jan. 14th, 1899."

The following is a summary of the sectional payments for work done:—

	Current A/c.			Special A/c.		
	£	s.	d.	£	s.	d.
Builder, Joiner, Plasterer, Slater, Tiler, &c.	327	0	0	440	0	0
Engineer, Smith, Plumber, Water Co., Corporation, Wireworker,	64	0	0	113	0	0
Painter, Paperhanger, Glazier, &c.	140	0	0	59	0	0
Furnisher, Electric Bells, &c. ...	3	0	0	46	0	0
Compensation for damage by Rain; Legal charges *re* neighbour's lights; Bank Interest	18	0	0	15	0	0
Architect's Commission	5	0	0	38	0	0
	£557	0	0	£711	0	0
Including 2 years maintenance, say at an average of £90	180	0	0	377	0	0
	£377	0	0	£1088	0	0

Thus by successive stages, from the simple Meeting House, established two centuries ago, have the growing requirements of the Congregation been met by the Friends of six generations; first for congregational worship, and then step by step for those agencies which are the natural out-growth of a living Church.

It will be interesting in the course of this brief history to inquire into the personel of the body, to see what manner of men and women they have been, so far as we can gather from the material at command, and how far the work attempted has witnessed a development at all abreast of the growth of the premises and the accommodation afforded.

The numbers in the plan of graves refer to list of burials in appendix.

THE QUAKER GRAVE-YARD.

Four straight brick walls, severely plain,
 A quiet city square surround;
A level space of nameless graves,—
 The Quakers' Burial-ground.

* * * *

To yon grim Meeting-house they fared,
 With thoughts as sober as their speech,
To voiceless prayer, to songless praise,
 To hear their elders preach.

Through quiet lengths of days they came,
 With scarce a change to this repose;
Of all life's loveliness they take
 The thorn without the rose.

S. WEIR MITCHELL.

Legacies and Trusts.

(Contributed by W. H. Holmes and T. Pumphrey.)

Though Newcastle Particular Meeting has never been rich in endowments for educational or charitable purposes, it will have been seen by the foregoing narrative of the growth of the premises that the money so expended has built up a property of increasing value in the very centre of the city.

At various times its tenure has been felt to be uncertain. In 1840 or 1841 it was proposed to carry a new street through it; and the late Richard Grainger at one time offered to build a new Meeting House for Friends on the site of St. Mary's R. C. Cathedral in West Clayton Street. This was strenuously opposed by George Richardson and others, and the scheme was abandoned.

Again, before building the Women's House and Class Rooms in 1868, the question of removal to other premises was seriously considered. At that time very few Friends resided at the North end of the town, and the Old Assembly Rooms in Westgate were spoken of as a good central position for the Meeting House. This proposal was also set aside in favour of the old premises.

The following statement was printed in 1886, in the Schedule of Trust Property, which may suitably find a place here:—

D

" The present premises in Pilgrim Street, Newcastle, came into possession of Friends in 1697 : the first Deed is dated 1600, and the meetings began to be held there in 1698. The site cost £120 : the buildings (no record) : in 1805 these were rebuilt for £1150 : in 1813 the House was enlarged at both ends at a cost of £347 ; in 1829 additional ground and buildings were purchased for £1644 : there was expended thereon £449 : in 1831 the warming apparatus cost £49 ; in 1832 a small piece of ground at the East End was granted free by the Corporation : in the following year the school rooms, Men's Meeting room (now included in the school room), wash-house, and offices were built, costing £1256 : in 1868 the Women's Meeting House and two class-rooms (now in one) were built, which together with approaches, enlargement of lobby, and other improvements, cost £2565 : in 1877 the internal alterations, already described, cost £206 : " and to this list must now be added the enlargement of the Mission Room and reconstruction of the Manors entrance £100 : alterations of the front premises in forming new committee room, &c., £388 : and lastly, in 1897, the building of new class rooms, enlargement of school room, reconstructing premises previously left off, levelling the floors right through, &c., £711.

In addition to the ground from Pilgrim Street to the Manors—say approximately 1840 square yards—the value of the buildings may be roughly put down (as insured) at £8500, viz. :—

1. Shops in Pilgrim Street with rooms over ... £1000
2. Principal Meeting House   1050
3. Caretaker's Dwelling House and adjuncts ...   500
4. Roofed Lobbies connecting these   800
5. Smaller Meeting House and Class Room A...   1800
6. Class Rooms B to I, School Room, Warehouse, &c.   3150
7. Lavatory and Fittings, &c.   200

The history of our modest monetary trusts may be thus recited :—

There is a sum of £160 now invested in Newcastle Corporation 3½ % Bonds, the history of which has some interest, thus :—

In 1742 Jeremiah Hunter made deed of gift of a house in Pandon, valued at £80,

> "To encourage industrious poor Friends, as Friends might see a service, that tho truly deserving might have the benefit."

In the same year a sum of £20 was given by Jane Middleton for the same purpose, which was expended in repairing said house in Pandon.

In the same year also a legacy of £40 was received under the will of Margaret Leighton

> "Unto the poor belonging to the congregation in Newcastle, vulgarly called Quakers, to be distributed as the Trustees or Managers of the said congregation may think fit."

The rent of the house, together with the interest on the legacy, were duly applied as directed until 1753, when, the monthly collections not being sufficient to support the charge on the meeting, they were appropriated to make up the deficiency, yet with a proper regard to the intention of the donors.

In 1769 a further legacy of £20 was left by James Christen

> "To the Trustees of the poor of the meeting of the people called Quakers in Newcastle-upon-Tyne for the use of the said poor."

In 1799 the house in Pandon was sold for £85, which (less expenses £5) was put out at interest, making with M. Leighton's and James Christen's legacies a total of £140.

Seven years later this money was called in and appropriated in aid of the fund for rebuilding the Meeting House; but on searching the minutes, in the following year, the true intentions of the donors were discovered, and the Preparative Meeting directed that £7 per annum should be taken out of the meeting's stock and applied as intended.

In 1821 the principal sum was replaced by Robert Ormston, thus relieving the current income of the meeting from the annual charge.

In the same year Robert Watson (of Newcastle, cabinet maker) bequeathed £50

"To be applied for such benevolent purposes and in such manner as the Friends of Newcastle shall think proper and direct."

£20 of this sum was accordingly added to the £140 already invested, thus completing the £160 now standing in Corporation Bonds in the names of Trustees.

The remainder of the £50 left by Robert Watson was spent as described in the Account Book of Newcastle Preparative Meeting.

In 1819 Joshua Watson left the sum of £50

"For the use of the particular meeting of Friends in Newcastle, to be disposed of as the said Meeting may see right and direct."

It was used in painting the Meeting House.

In 1832 Ann Rawlinson bequeathed by will the sum of £40

"To the poor belonging to the Quaker's Meeting at Newcastle-upon-Tyne."

It was distributed amongst poor Friends.

In 1808 John Patterson, "late of Newcastle-upon-Tyne, whitesmith," directed by his will that the sum of £300

"Be paid to the Trustees for the time being, of the Society of Friends, commonly called Quakers, in Newcastle-upon-Tyne, to be by such Trustees placed out at interest, and the interest thereof to be applied to such purposes in aid of the funds of the Society as the Trustees for the time being of the said Society may think fit."

This sum is secured upon the property in Pilgrim Street at $4\frac{1}{2}\%$ and the interest paid to the Preparative Meeting's Treasurer by the Property Committee, thus yielding £13 10s. per annum towards the current expenses for relief, education, &c., of the Preparative Meeting.

In 1896 Ellen Richardson left £100

"To the Newcastle-upon-Tyne Preparative Meeting of the Society of Friends for the use of their Meeting House."

This was allotted to the fund then being devoted to the formation of the Committee Rooms over the front shops in Pilgrim Street.

In the yearly accounts of "the Property Committee" an item occurs which has a curious history, which will probably be little understood even by local Friends

It is entered in the accounts as "Ground rent to the Trustees of Hanover Square Chapel." It would be more correctly described as a rent-charge. The following explanation has been kindly furnished, in answer to enquiry, by Richard Welford, M.A. :—

Gosforth, Newcastle-upon-Tyne, *Feby. 24th, 1899.*

DEAR SIR,—Replying to your favour, I have the pleasure to inform you that Barbara Gee, of Newcastle, widow, by a will in my possession, dated March 19, 1724-5, left her property in Pilgrim Street (and elsewhere) in trust to her executors, as follows :—

"Whereas my son, John Gee, late of Newcastle-upon-Tyne, gentleman, deceased, did by his last will and testament in writing, duly executed, charge all the said messuages, &c. (in Pilgrim Street) after my death, with the yearly payment of the sum of six pounds for ever to such person or persons as should at the time of my death be minister or ministers of and for the Protestant Dissenters' meeting-house for religious worship, situate without the Close Gate, without the walls, but within the libertys of the said town of New-castle, and to the successor and successors of such minister for ever, I do hereby certify and confirm the said devise of six pounds per annum for ever, and do hereby order and appoint that the said sum bo paid by four equal quarterly payments yearly and every year to the hands of the said minister and his successors for ever. And I hereby make all the said premises liable to the payment of the said six pounds per annum for ever, to be paid as aforesaid to the said minister and his successors whether the said meeting-house be at the Close Gate or elsewhere."

Yours very truly,

RICHARD WELFORD.

Local Records of Friends.

"Your papers are too long, give me a short paper."—

JUDGE JEFFERIES to MARGARET FELL FOX.

THE records of the Society of Friends are voluminous, and in a "short paper," an idea of their extent, nature, and variety only can be given. These records arise in several ways. Friends have claimed, for instance, the right to solemnise marriages in the method they deemed scriptural and reasonable; and they recognised the fact that they should faithfully record them. Registrations of birth, marriage, and burial have been carried out for centuries. And the Society has, at most of its centres, its history told in its minutes. For nearly 250 years, minutes of the business of the meetings have been kept; and in the books of the Monthly and Quarterly gatherings there is much interesting matter. The local records include the books of "Goatshead" and Newcastle Monthly Meetings from 1674 down to the present time; and the Newcastle Preparative (or local) books from the year 1707, with certificates of removal, and similar documents. These volumes and documents are partly in duplicate—for the men's meeting, and that of the women; they are naturally guarded with care; for they include probably the fullest church records of any denomination in the city. The earliest of these is that of the minute-books of the men's meeting of Goatshead, and Newcastle. The small folio book is extant, which gives the minutes of the Monthly Meeting "from 1674 to 1707." This precious little volume differs much from the minute books to-day. Its clasps are worn off; the ink is occasionally faded, the ruling is irregular. There is no name of the clerk given; none of representatives; there is no record in it of birth or death; and a few pages at the close are devoted to summaries of accounts. The spelling lacks monotony—we have " Sheils," " Sheilds," and " Shields," " Gateside," " Goatshead," and " Goateshead." There is no indication of the numbers present. The first minute is as follows :—

> " At the Monthly Meeting at Gotsheade, 9th of 9th month, 1674, Thomas Merryman, of South Shields, in the county of Durham, propounded his Intention of taking mary neale, of ye same, spinster, to be his wife; a certificate received from the said mary Neale's ffather giving his consent. Thomas Chandler and Robert Curry to make further inquiry."

At the next Monthly Meeting, the second propounding of intention took place, and the two persons were freed to marry. The meeting seems to have been largely occupied with matters relating to marriage proposals, records being frequent. In 1698, 4th month, when Newcastle meeting house was in progress, John Tizack, of Howdon Pans, and Dorothy Heslam ; Joseph Johnson and Sarah Fisher; and Israel Brown (master mariner) and Joan Linton were " before meeting" at one time. To the last the minute book records frequent proposals. The Meeting at Newcastle 8th of 10th month, 1707, has first the case before it of Jervas Leighton and Susannah Hildreth, and " find nothing but that they are clear," so they were liberated. It had also the intentions of William Moor and Sarah Sanderson, and of Robert Dixon and Jane Rogers, so that the marriage market was brisker two centuries ago than now.

There were cases of " marrying out." In 1678, Robert and Jean Linton were appointed to wait on Jane Mitchell " touching her Intention to marry one of the World," but the visit was unsuccessful, for a few months later a further appointment was needed to visit Jane " on her Marriage contrary to Truth." About the same time Cuthbert Johnson was remonstrated with. He said " he did not know any evil he had done in marrying a woman that is not a ffriend," whereupon the clerk wrote him that "ffriends judges thy condition to be very sad," but Cuthbert "continued obstinate," and so passes out of knowledge.

Burials at times concerned the Meeting. On the 13th of 10th month, 1675, at Gateside:

"ffriends have generally given their judgment touching Burialls, that when there is a Coffin, there's no necessity for any cloth [cover] at all."

In 1708, the "many gravestones that Shields Friends have in their burying ground," caused concern, and their removal was ordered "with consent of parties concerned." Shields Friends did not wish to remove them, but said they would discontinue the practice of putting them up.

The last minute of the first volume of minutes is— the Quarterly Meetings

"Queeries have been read over and severally answered by a member of each meeting. Lancelot Wardell, Benjamin Atkinson, and Caleb Tennant are desired to carry the account thereof to the Quarterly Meeting."

This is probably the *first locally recorded* appointment of what are now called representatives to the higher Church Assembly.

The early records of church officials are few, but Thomas Wilkinson and Jeremiah Hunter were appointed in 1683 to take the care of recording marriages, births, and burials. There is scarcely a reference to Elders, by that name. The first minute as to overseers is in 1699. The question was one of appointing "some Friends in each Meeting to inspect ye conversation of Friends" in their respective Meetings, and it was considered that "a general care is preferrable to a particular" one. Still for unity's sake they would put the proposal into practice; and in the 4th month, 1699, Sunderland Friends report that they have appointed Wm. Maud and Lance. Wardell. Shields appointed John Buston and Thomas Raylton, and Newcastle Geo. Raw and Benjamin Atkinson.

We may now give a series of extracts from these records, which will show the scope and method of the work of the church in its early years on the Tyne, premising that the distinction was not so clearly drawn then as it now is between the functions of the different gatherings :—

Schools.—In 1708, the Monthly Meeting appointed "Samuel Maud, John Freeman, Jeremiah Hunter, Joshua Middleton, Caleb Tennant, and Thomas Fearon to visit the School Masters and Mistresses belonging to this meeting " . . . . "according to the directions of the Quarterly Meeting." In the same year "the want of a School Master or Mistress that is a Friend at Shields" was noted. Shields Friends, on being asked, were desirous that such a Friend "might be settled amongst them."

Ministers' Certificates.—Lancelot Wardell, in 1713, "laid before the Meeting his Intention of visiting Friends in some parts of Yorkshire, Lancashire, and Elsewhere and Desiring a Certificate from this meeting, it is accordingly granted, ffriends having Unity with him therein."

In 1727, Lancelot Wardell desired and obtained a certificate of Friends' unity with "his Concern to visit Friends in some parts of this Nation." He returned it in 3rd month, 1728, with a "comfortable account of his journey."

In 1759, Edward Walton had a certificate to visit "Friends in Ireland and Scotland." He returned it in 9th month, reporting the visit as having "been very much to his own Satisfaction and Comfort."

The "Select Meeting."—In 1709, it was asked that "one or two Friends that are not concerned in a Publick Testimony in Friends' Meeting be acquainted from every monthly meeting to attend the Select meeting of ministering Friends," and on the 12th of 10th month, William Midford and James Gibson are so appointed.

In 1723, it is described *first* as a "Quarterly Select Meeting of Ministering Friends *and Elders*."

In 1739, a "Select Meeting" for each Monthly
Meeting was begun, the first local one being in 3rd month
at Sunderland, five representatives from the Monthly
Meeting being appointed to it.

Marriage contrary to rule.—In 1728, Elizabeth Marshall
and Mary Robinson were reported as "married from among
Friends," and to clear "ye Truth's Testimony" Reginald
Holme and John Freeman were to draw up testimonies
against them. Very many such testimonies are recorded,
the wording often beginning: "A Testimony against Ann
Fallowfield for outrunning to a Priest, and joining with
marriage with one of another Persuasion."

In 1751, Ann Shotton sent a paper to the Monthly
Meeting "signifying her sorrow for having disobliged
Friends by marrying contrary to the rules of our Society,"
and she was again "received into fellowship" after enquiry.

Admission into Membership.—About 1756, Joseph King,
the son of members of Stockton Meeting, served his
"apprenticeship to the sea." with John Heath, of Whitby, a
"man that is not a Friend." It was thought he became a
member of Whitby Meeting ; but he was not known to
Whitby Friends, the ship he sailed in frequenting other
ports. Stockton Monthly Meeting was "applyd to," but
they excused themselves from giving a certificate, though
recommending Newcastle to admit him. After enquiring
of his employer, Newcastle Meeting sets forth the facts.
and says it has "*condescended* to admit him a member,"
and soon after Joseph King marries Hannah Shaw, at
Shotton.

Poor George Raw.—In 8th month, 1755, a certificate
for George Raw (woolcomber) and family, who have
removed to Durham, was "read, signed by the Clerk,
and given to George Wakefield, jun., to send to Durham
Friends." Two months later, Durham Friends claim
£1/6/6½, which they had laid out through the illness
and death of George Raw's wife, and this was paid by

Newcastle Meeting. In 1756, Durham Friends returned George Raw's certificate, and Newcastle Friends arranged to apprentice his oldest son to John Clark, of Sunderland, "baker and tallow chandler," and it was proposed the younger son should be sent to "Friends' Workhouse, London," but the father objected. George's intemperance brings him some reproof, but in 1758, George Raw and Mary Little were cleared for marriage.

Newcastle Infirmary.—The Quarterly Meeting at Durham recommended "a generous Collection to be made in each Particular Meeting" for the Infirmary at Newcastle. In the list of original subscribers towards the building of this Infirmary, in 1751, the result is seen in an acknowledgement: "Quarterly Meeting of people called Quakers, Durham, £70."

"*Well to be off with the old Love.*"—In 1748, "William Chapman. of Whitby, and Hannah Baines published their intentions of marriage with each other;" no fewer than seven Friends were appointed to enquire into their "clearness from other engagements," Benjamin Ward having complained of the lady's conduct. The enquirers reported that she was "not clear;" Hannah Baines sent to the Monthly Meeting a paper acknowledging that there "had been a Treaty on foot betwixt me and Benjamin Ward," but she embraced the offer of "another person" through some report, and regretted her fault. In the end she was set free for marriage with William Chapman.

Testimonies to Ministers.—On the death of some prominent ministers, the Meeting recorded its appreciation of their labours and their lives. Thus the death of William Maude, in 1730, is the occasion of one of the first of such testimonies. He is described as "Our Worthy and well-beloved Friend William Maude, of Sunderland," and his "exemplary Life and Conversation, his Qualifications in the Truth," and his "eminent Services in the Church and

Ministry" are noticed. The Testimony was "given to Reginald Holme to be tendered to the Yearly Meeting in London." Again, "A Testimony on behalf of our worthy Friend. Jeremiah Hunter, deceased," was read at the Monthly Meeting in 1741-2, and was ordered to be sent to the Quarterly Meeting; and in somewhat similar wording a Testimony as to Archibald Gillespy was endorsed in 1756.

Sufferings.—Very frequently reports are received about the sufferings of Friends. In 1721, the report is concise: "Newcastle Friends have brought in their Sufferings. Shields Friends give an account that they have none. Sunderland Friends not having theirs ready, are ordered to bring them in to the next Meeting."

Thus far, the extracts have been nearly all from the records of the Monthly Meeting, embracing Newcastle, Sunderland, and vicinity. There are, as we have said, minutes also for the Preparative Meeting, which included the smaller area around Newcastle. Its work and method may be shown in a similar manner:—

Accounts.—The first statement given of accounts of Newcastle Preparative Meeting is for 1706-7, the payments being £8/11/10½ (including £3/12/0 for "4 of George Fox's book"); and the collections and 10/0 for "a year's rent for yard" brought in £9/12/9. Expenses include items such as "setting a Friend to Alnwick, with horse hire, 11/6." To "John Simpson for tabling" [board]. "Gravemaking" is usually paid for by 1/0; "Wm. Ramsay's son for one year's scooling, 10/0"; "horse hire for a friend to Shields, 2/0; to hay and oats for Friends' horses, £1/2/7."

Settlements.—As instancing the difficulty the old laws of settlement gave, an example may be given. In 1722, "John Farer & Robert Westgarth are desired to visit John Watson to enquire into his circumstances," and if needed to give him relief. A month later, "Jeremiah Hunter & Wm. Midford" are desired to "write to ffriends of Embleton

Meeting relating to John Watson." Two months later Jeremiah Hunter reports that he has seen an influential Embleton Friend thereon, and written further. " The issue thereof is left till an Answer be returned." Later, again, a further appointment is made to write to Embleton Friends. An unsatisfactory reply is spoken of; an answer to it is given; and finally in 1723, the matter ends; John Watson receiving relief from Newcastle.

Women Friends.—In 1708. "itt is ordered that Wm. Little and Wm. Dove give twenty shillings to the women Friends for the use of Mary Ellet, and that they send twenty shillings more to Sarah Cutter." In 1714, the Meeting ordered £1 to be put into the hands of one or more women Friends, " to encourage the Service of women Friends," to distribute as they think fit.

Clothing.—A minute with a humorous side states that it is agreed, in 1716, that " Benj. Atkinson do get a Coat and Britches for Geo: Martin, and demand ye money from ye Stock." It is worth adding that in 1717 in the accounts of the Meeting there is the charge of 10/4 for "cloath for Coate and a pair of Breaches for George Martin." As Benjamin Atkinson was a tailor, and only charged for the " cloath," it is possible that he did the work for his poor Friend without charge.

Treasurers.—From various minutes we find that the early treasurers for Newcastle Preparative Meeting were, in 1708, Wm. Little and Wm. Dove; in 1712, Thomas Shields and Jacob Watson; and in 1718, " John Fayrer is desired to assist Thomas Shields in keeping acct. of this Meeting's Stock."

Overseers.—The overseers were more frequently changed. Those for Newcastle Preparative Meeting are given over many years. The first minute in its records, in 1707, says: " Robert Westgarth and Thomas Hodgson hath att Friends' request taken upon thems. ye Oversight of truth's affairs." In 1709. " Robert Westgarth & Thomas

Hodgson desired to be released;" and in 1710, William Midford and Isaac Hunter were appointed to succeed them. In 1712, John Fayrer and Joshua Middleton, jun., appointed to take the oversight in place of W. Midford & J. Hunter, released; in 1713, John Fayrer and George Raw; in 1714, Thomas Hodgson and John Francis; in 1717, Benjamin Atkinson and Wm. Little.

In 1720, Robert Westgarth and Isaac Hunter are desired to take upon themselves the Inspection of Friends' Conversation. In the 4th month, they are desired to make enquiry as to the reason of the frequent differences between John Moore and his wife. On their report a Testimony against John Moore was issued for his "un-Truth like conduct to his Wife." The great provocation of speech she gave is noticed; but, making no profession with Friends, she is left to "the Church she pretends to be a member of."

In 1723, John Middleton and Thomas Shields were "appointed to take upon themselves the Oversight of Friends." So the story would go on, until in later years the appointment of the overseers becomes one of the functions of the Monthly Meeting.

Briefs.—To Newcastle Preparative Meeting many appeals for help came, such as for sufferers by "Fire at Littleport, Isle of Ely," and in reply 7/6 was ordered to be given. In 1708 "A collection has been made to the briefs for the Sufferers at Lisburn, and there is given to itt £1/7/3." And there are scores of instances of relief given from the funds for cases of loss.

Representatives.—Newcastle Preparative Meeting appointed representatives thus: "Monthly Meeting falls at Shields,—Jeremiah Hunter and Joshua Middleton are desired to attend it;" but when the "Monthly Meeting falls at ys. Place," no representatives were appointed,— possibly because a general attendance was expected of Friends in the town.

Women Friends' Meetings.

In 1691, London Yearly Meeting advised the encouragement of "faithful Women's Meetings, and the settling of them where they are wanting," the duties being defined. The minutes of the Newcastle Monthly Meeting of Women Friends are extant from 1694. Preceding the first minute are Epistles from the Women's Quarterly and Monthly Meetings, the first of which has the signatures of "Joan Linton," of Shields; "Jane ffisher (Gateshead); and others. "Our sisters att Raby Monthly Meeting" send to the Quarterly Meeting at Durham, a communication it "thought fitt," the pith of which is that when "ffriends have daughters com'd and coming up to Marredg State, we do desire that parents may in the Love of God carefully advise their Children that when any young man's Preposell to them in relation to marridg, they may be cautious in not giving incurredgment to any, Least they draw out their affections after them until they have seriously Weighed the same." This letter, signed "on behalf of ye Monthly Meeting by me, Mary Stoutal," was sent down by Durham Quarterly Meeting to the Men's Meeting at Gateshead, there read, signed by "Joshua Middleton," and recommended to the particular meetings. The last Epistle is from the Women's Yearly Meeting in London, 1694, "ye Sallutation of our Dear Love to you, Tender Sisters," admonishes them to live in innocent love, to take care "in apparell and behaviour in all to be good examples to children and servants."

The first minute, "att our Women's Monthly Meeting at Gateside, ye 10th day of ye 10th month, 1694," is :—

Arthur Dixinson, of Whitby, acquainted this Meeting wth his Intentions of Marridge wth Joanna Trewhitt, of Sunderland, to wch she likewise gave her Consent. Deborah Wardell and Rachel Maude are appointed to Make Enquiry concerning her, and to give an Acct. to ye next Monthly Meeting.

And at the next meeting, the account being favourable, " they are left to their Liberty to proceed according to ye Order of Truth." The Intentions of Anthony Robinson and Sarah Peale, of "Coulercotes;" of Isaac Fallowfeald and Alcey Corneath; of Zephaniah Haddock and Eleanor Dove; of Samuel Cooper and Sarah Groves, are rehearsed, with many others. Minutes such as these form the chief part of the early records of Women Friends. When the parties are clear, "they are Left to Accomplish their Marriage according to the Good Order of Truth." When the intended bride does not belong to the local meeting "its Left to Men Friends" to enquire as to the clearness.

There are copied into the minute book of Women Friends, the early advices for the sex issued from Durham in 1709, urging them to attend the Meetings for Worship regularly and punctually, and "also to give their Servants what liberty they can to go to Meetings." They are advised to be careful to keep out all "needless and superfluous fashions as yt. of cutting and powdering the hair" and having "our Hoods over high, and making Manties with over wide sleeves, short Laps, and too much to pin up behind," but to aim at being "adorned in modest Apparel." To keep to plainness in furniture, to avoid "furbiloing their Bed Vallances and Window Curtains," or .any such "foolish and unnecessary custom." To visit Friends and neighbours in times of affliction and sickness; to be circumspect to keep from drowsiness in times of Meetings; and that "women who keep Shops be careful to observe justice in weights and measures."

Women Friends naturally had overseers of their own sex, the first definitely named being for Newcastle, Ann Midford, and Sarah Hunter; and they are asked to " Bring in an Accountt of their Care in Matters Relateing to that Concern," which seems to have been satisfactory.

The cash accounts of Women Friends are clearly kept. The receipts are "From the Men's Meeting," and "Collected at our Women's Meeting," whilst the payments are usually such as "given to Jane Wear, by Friends;" to "Sweeping the Meeting House, 2/6;" "disbursed on Kattrina Ellot's burial, 17/9." Sarah Hunter seems to have been one of the earliest Treasurers for Women Friends; and later, Rebecca Airey.

Discipline of the Society.

THE "Discipline" includes all "those arrangements and regulations which are instituted for the civil and religious benefit" of the Society. When the Friends began to connect themselves in the bond of religious fellowship they were "engaged to admonish, encourage," and "watch over and help one another in love." Gradually meetings for these purposes were added to the meetings of worship; and whilst the "care of the churches falls upon all the members," it was felt that the gifts of ministry and of oversight should be recognised when appreciated. Hence the commencement of "meetings for discipline," with many duties—to care for the poor, to see to the education of the youth, to admonish members who became unruly, to record births, marriages, and deaths, to testify against offenders. From time to time, as needed, the various meetings of Friends issued such advices of warning and encouragement as they thought needed. These advices and rules of the highest court, the yearly meeting, were circulated at first by written copies; but in 1783 a series of Extracts from them was printed, a later edition of which received the title of the "Rules of Discipline of the Religious Society of Friends." These rules, or advices, varied as the needs of passing years suggest, are the methods on which the discipline works. If a member is about to be married, his procedure should be in accordance with the now simple rules. In earlier days, the intended bridegroom and bride "declared their intention of marriage" in both the meetings of men and women friends, and if the parents or guardians were not present, their written consent was needed. Here is such a certificate of consent from Jannett Graham, whose daughter Ann was to be united to Rowland Wilson :—

6th of ye 6th mo., 1710.

This may certifie unto all whom it may concern that I doe give my free consent that my daughter Ann doe marry with Rowland Wilson. As witness my hand ye day and year aforesd.

JANNETT GRAHAM.

Witnesses

SAMUEL CLANE.
ROBERT LATIMER.

When, in due course, the marriage had been solemnised a Certificate was given, in which it was recited that the two persons had declared their intentions "before several publick meetings of the People of God called Quakers," and their proceedings having been approved by the said meetings, they "appeared in a Public Assembly of the aforesaid People, and others, met together for that end and purpose, and according to the Example of the Holy Men of God recorded in the Scriptures of Truth," did take each other as man and wife, and "did then and there to these Presents set their Hands." The ancient certificate we have partly copied from, is dated in the "ninth moneth, called November, in the year, according to the English account, One Thousand Six Hundred Eighty and Six," and the wording of the certificate is little altered in essentials down to to-day.

Where the intended bridegroom and bride belonged to different districts or meetings, there were enquiries needed in both ; and the copy below, of an olden document, shows how this was done :—

"From our Monthly Meeting held at Scarborough (in Yorkshire) this first day of the 7th mo., 1724.

To Friends of the Monthly Meeting at Newcastle (in Northumberland). These :—

Whereas Our Friend, George Wakefield, Jun. (late a Member of our meeting, but now of yours), hath by Letter requested our Certificate concerning his clearness from all other women in respect to marriage, except Ann Robinson, a member of your sd meeting.

We, therefore, hereby certifie you (or whom else it may concern) yt after due enquiry made by the Friends appointed at our last Monthly Meeting, we do not find but yt he is free and clear in relation to marriage except with the sd Ann Robinson. So with dear love we conclude and remain yr. Friends and Brethren in the Truth.

Signed in and on behalf of our said meeting by

Reuben Linskell	Robt. Garbutt	George Wilson
Robt. Henderson	John Garbutt	Robert Mothersdill
Jno. Bland	Robt. Hopperson	Jos. Smithies
Hugh Pravis	Isaac Skelton	Wm. Goffee
Fra. Salkeld	Jno. Langstaffe	Robt. Moller, sen.
	Jos. Sergeant."	

There were some Friends who married "contrary to rule," and thus came under the "Discipline." In these cases, there was in the early days the result we have seen—they "were excluded from fellowship." "Testimonies" were given forth against them, and published occasionally. Usually these "testimonies" began by stating that the person concerned had been "in fellowship with us in profession of the Truth," and had let out his or her "affections to one not of our profession," and had "outrun to a Priest to be married," the meeting testified against such "disorderly walking," and deemed the offender "out of unity" until he or she repented. That repentance was often shown in a paper such as this:—

Friends, it hath been a great trouble to me that I should Have gone, contrary to the principle of Truth which I bless God that I am made sencible is right. which if I had kept their I had been preserved from running out to a priest to be married, which I hartely repent of that action. Friends my desire is that I may be in unity with you as in time past, also that you will be as tender as truth will allow so that by God's assistance and your friendships I may be made to keep my place for the time to come.

So I remain your Friend,

ELLENOR ROBSON.

13th 9 mo., 1720.

One of the most cautious certificates is from Stockton Meeting given to a Friend who requested one to enable him to be "cleared" for marriage. Stockton Meeting, in 1736, thus certified him to Newcastle, stating that "Daniel Calvert was by birth and education a member of our meeting, and collected [that is, met] with us several years. We

believe he was not guilty of Prophane Language neither
that he would knowingly deceive or defraud." As it was
several years since he left Stockton, during which years he
had resided at or near Sunderland, his "Conduct and Conversation of late years must be better known to Friends
there than to us."

As time passed, however, these certificates of transfer
grew more frequent in number and similar in wording.
One sent to Newcastle from Darlington in 1777, on behalf
of Sarah Dale, is written almost with copper plate clearness,
and states that she left "clear of debt and marriage
engagements." Those who recommend her "to your care"
include Mary Pease, Mary Flounders, Jane Backhouse, and
Eliz. Pease; Edward Pease, John Stephenson, Joseph
Proctor, James Backhouse, Jona. Backhouse, John Flounders,
and others.

In the same way, when a trader could not pay his just
debts, a testimony against him was issued. When a Friend
habitually neglected meetings, there was a similar course,—
in all cases after private admonition and enquiry.

Again, and in a more pleasant method, the "discipline"
becomes apparent. When a Minister felt it called of him
to travel in the Work of the Ministry, he placed his desires
and prospects before his Friends in the appointed meetings;
and, if they concurred, they granted him a Certificate.
Elizabeth Johnson, in 1784, for instance, desired and
obtained such a minute for religious service in "Yorkshire,
Nottinghamshire, or elsewhere," which simply expressed
"good Unity with her gift in the Ministry," and trusted
that its faithful exercises might be to the edification of those
she visited. It was signed on behalf of Newcastle Monthly
Meeting, by Jeremiah Hunter, Lancelot Wardell, Warren
Maude, Jon: Raine, and 29 other Friends. Similarly, in
1786, Edward Walton felt a concern upon his mind to visit
some meetings in Westmoreland, and he received a Certificate
showing the good Unity his Friends had with him, and

expressing the hope that "he may return to us with peace in his bosom."

Later Certificates include those of George Richardson to Ireland, to many Counties in England and Wales; to Rachael Priestman, and others. One of the Certificates to George Richardson has no fewer than 59 signatures; another on the occasion of Rachael Priestman's visit to Cornwall is signed by 58 Friends. For many years "Guides" were provided to accompany visiting Ministers and to relieve them of part of the trouble of arrangement of time and method of travelling. A list of guides for Newcastle is before us in writing. It defines the duties, and shows that for 1814 there were in all 18—William Beaumont, John Bowron, Hadwen Bragg, John Branting-ham, Anthony Clapham, Timothy Cutforth, John Foster, James Gilpin, Daniel Oliver, Jonathan Priestman, George Richardson, E. Robinson, Joseph Rooke, W. Rowntree, John Watson. Jun., Joshua Watson, Jun., W. Wilson, and Edward Wright.

The purposes of the discipline were largely aided by the answering of queries meant to ascertain the conditions of the constituent meetings. Begun about 1682 with three questions, they were increased in number later. At first the answers were verbal, then partly in writing and partly verbally; and later entirely in writing. In 1761, after a visit from Samuel Fothergill, Willm. Dilworth, Isaac Wilson, Jonathan Raine, John Lindow, Joseph Taylor, Thomas Corbyn, and William Chapman, the answers to the queries appear in the Monthly Meeting minute book.

The answers show the nature of the queries then sent down. Meetings were duly attended. Love and unity are in a good degree preserved. Care was taken to "train up the youth in a Godly Conversation." The "testimony against Tythes, Priests' demands," and other ecclesiastical imposts was kept up. Most Friends were clear of frequenting places of diversion. Friends appeared just in their dealings. Care was taken to advise such as "incline to marry contrary to the rules." Friends were "deputed to take care of the oversight" in each meeting. "And, lastly, the poor are provided for, and "proper care is taken of the Education of their Offspring."

The doorkeepers fulfil a useful place in the economy of meetings for discipline. In the olden days their duties were defined with exactness so complete that the time of "lighting of the candles" is stated, and provision is made for their "snuffing in as quiet a manner as possible." Many a good citizen did first public service as doorkeeper in Pilgrim Street Meeting.

The Sufferings of Friends.

Reference has already been made to, and examples given of, some of the personal sufferings of members of the Society of Friends in the maintenance of liberty of conscience. Refusal to take oath, refusal to uncover the head before dignitaries, refusal to do any military service, and refusal to pay ecclesiastic demands, brought heavy sufferings on the Quakers.

These denials were not the result of obstinacy. They were based in some cases on the command of Christ; as, for instance, "Swear not at all," and others on equally well-known Biblical injunctions. As time went on, the law was altered, and the affirmation was allowed to Friends, so that some of the causes of imprisonment were removed. Distraints for tithes, church rates, and similar demands, were long continued. The Society decided that records of these should be kept, and thousands of such cases are recorded. It may be sufficient to extract from the scores that are locally kept, a statement for a few years, and to give one or two examples of the nature. The distraints on Newcastle Friends about a hundred years ago included in

				Amount.
				£ s. d.
1779	Andrew Oliver and Thomas Wigham, farmers	...		6 16 9
1785	Andrew Oliver, Benwell Hills	...	... ...	3 13 2
1786	Do.	do.	... ...	1 13 6
1787	Do.	do.	... ...	2 12 6
1788	Do.	do.	... ...	13 13 6
1790	Do.	do.	... ...	2 4 0
1792	Do.	do.	... ...	1 6 0
1796	Do.	do.	... ...	2 18 0
1798	Do.	do.	... ...	2 0 0

In ten years the sum of £39 4s. 11d. was thus taken from Andrew Oliver.

James King, of the Low Glasshouses, appears to have had a farm at West Kenton, and from him, in 1779, there was taken £6 9s. 9d. From his relative William King, of West Kenton, in seven years, £81 6s. 10d. was taken; from John Raw, of West Brunton, £85 15s. 6d. was taken in seven years; from Ralph Bainbridge, of Gateshead, distraints in two years took £3 6s. 1d.; from David Sutton, in 1788, £1 3s. 8d. was taken; from Hadwen Bragg, in three years, the sum of £11 7s. 3d. was taken apparently for re-building "All Saints' Steeplehouse"; and from Anthony Clapham £7 12s. 6d. Let us give, in the quaint wording of the past, a few illustrations that also show something of Newcastle of the past.

" Taken from Andrew Oliver, of Benwell Hills, in the parish of St. John's, and County of Northumberland, for several years Tythes of Potatoes and various small Tythes (amounting to £7 11s. 11d., and £1 13s. 6d. charges) demanded by ——— Lushington, Vicar of Newcastle, under a Warrant, signed Thos. Fenwick and T. Charles Bigge, Justices, and Henry Sanderson, Constable, 12th of 9th mo., 1788. The sd Henry Sanderson took ten Pykes of Hay value £10 10s.; 13th of same month, taken also from the sd. Andrew Oliver for Tythe in Kind by Mary Curry's Servant, Tythe Farmer, Mathw. White Ridley, Impropriator, 18 Stooks and 3 Shiefs of Oats value 2/- each...

2/- each...	£1 16	6
17th of same month, 7 Stooks and 9 Shiefs of Maslin	1 7	0
Total taken for Tithe in kind ...	3 3	6
By Justices' Warrant ...	10 10	0
In all	£13 13	6

Witness, John Trummell."

"Tithe in Kind taken away from John Raw, of West Brunton, in the parish of Gosforth, in the County of Northumberland, by Thos. Tod, Tythe Farmer, Matthew White Ridley, Impropriator, 1783. Taken away the Eleventh Day of the Ninth Month, three Thrave and eight Sheaves of Wheat, value at eight shillings ℣ Thrave £1 6 8

Ditto Nine Thrave and Twenty-two Sheaves of Barly value at four shillings ℣ Thrave 1 19 8

Taken away the Sixteenth Day of the Ninth Month, Eighteen Thrave and Twelve Sheave of Oats, value at four shillings ℣ Thrave 3 14 0

Taken away the Seventeenth day of the Ninth Month, Eighteen Thrave of Oats, value do. 3 12 0

Taken away the Twentieth day of the Ninth Month, Six Thrave of Barly, value at two shillings ℣ Thrave 0 12 0

£11 4 4

Witness, Robert Oliver."

"Tythe in kind taken from John Raw, of West Brunton, in the county of Northumberland, and parish of Gosford, by Thomas Todd, Tythe Farmer, Mathew White Ridley, Impropriator.

1796, Thomas Todd took away the 13th day of the 9th month, 16 Stooks of Wheat at 4 shillings a Stook £3 4 0

Took away the 19th day of the 9th month 34 Stooks of Barly at 2 shillings a Stook 3 8 0

Took away the 1st day of the 10th month 120 Stooks of Oats at 1 shilling and 6 pence a Stook ... 9 0 0

In all £15 12 0

Witness, George Moore."

"Newcastle, 21st of Fifth Month, 1790. Taken from Jno. Patterson on Acct. of Building the New Steple House, by a Warrent Granted by Hugh Hornby, Mayor, and Willm. ——, Cramlington, Aldmn.

Richd. Hill and Thoas. Annet, Serjents, came and Took away Silver Plate and sold it, the Demand was.. ... ... £6 16 6

The Serjent Charges 0 5 0

£7 1 6

Witness, Eunice Gibson."

"Distraint from Hadwen Bragg, Newcastle-Tyne, 4th Mo., 17th, 1798.

1 ps. yd. wide Linen, 25 ys. @ 2/9 ... ... £3 8 9

For Church cess, claimed under the general warrant issued for the re-building All Saints'.

Geo. Scaife, Churchwarden.

Witness, Joseph Rooke."

The Sufferings thus illustrated may have their extent indicated by the statement that in 1762, it was reported that " Corn tythe " was taken from five Newcastle Friends to the value of £35 17s. 6d. ; one Shields Friend, John Richardson, of Seahill (Earsdon Parish) suffered to the extent of £19 13s. 6d. In 1764, the amounts were Newcastle Friends, £53 1s. 6d. ; Shields Friends, £18 11s. 3½d.; but the account was made up before Sunderland Friends had been " distrained on," as they expected to be. In 1770, the total for the three places is given as £69 5s. 3d.

For two centuries, Members of the Society of Friends suffered much financially. In this century, several laws that pressed harshly upon them were repealed, and the Society has ceased to record the sufferings. The chief of the meetings that had charge of the recording and alleviation of persecuted Quakers—the " Meeting for Sufferings " has had its time occupied in later years with attempts to mitigate the sufferings of other people.

Recollections of Newcastle Meeting Sixty Years Ago.

Contributed by William Harris Robinson.

My recollections of Newcastle Meeting date mainly from the closing months of 1836, when I returned home from Ackworth school. I have one however of an earlier date, connected with the Meeting House premises. I recollect being taken when quite a child to the caretakers house, which then fronted into Pilgrim Street, to see from the upper rooms a great procession pass along the street. This was the triumphal entry into Newcastle of the successful candidates at the great Northumberland election of 1826 on their return from Alnwick, the county town.

The large Meeting House used then to be divided by a screen or partition stretching from the door to the opposite wall and above the screen was a gallery or "Loft" as it was called. The screen was furnished with moveable shutters which could be opened at will, or closed when two rooms were required. The men's meeting for business was held in the lower part under the "loft," and that of the women in the upper part of the house. When the new buildings at the foot of the grave-yard were completed, accommodation was found there for the men's meeting and the partition dividing the large Meeting House was removed. The "loft" however remained until recent years, and until its condition was deemed unsafe. Later on a new Meeting House has been built for the use of our lady friends, with several classrooms and other apartments for the convenience and greater efficiency of the Sabbath School. In 1836, Meetings for Worship were held on Sundays, at ten in the morning and at three in the afternoon, the week-day meeting at ten on Wednesday morning. The experiment of holding the afternoon meeting on Sundays at four p.m. was tried for a time but was soon discontinued and the old hour of three p.m. resumed. This continued to be the hour for many years until the time was changed to the evening. The Meeting House was not then lighted with gas and in the afternoons of winter as the light waned it was the duty of the doorkeeper to light a dozen or more candles fixed in a chandelier suspended from the ceiling.

I remember being present at several interments in the grave-yard but on the completion of the Westgate Hill cemetery, burials in the grave-yard became fewer until it was finally closed by Act of Parliament. There has however been one interment since, that of George Richardson; but to enable that to be done the consent of the Home Secretary was obtained.

Looking back to 1836, the Ministers who sat in the gallery facing the meeting were George Richardson, Margaret Bragg, Daniel Oliver, and Jonathan and Rachel Priestman. Another Friend, John Reed Seekings, frequently took vocal part in meetings and he was acknowledged as a Minister shortly before he removed to Birmingham.

George Richardson at that time was the most influential Friend in the Meeting. He had travelled much as a Minister and was well known amongst Friends in other parts of the country. After retiring from business he resided in Albion Street, and there for many years devoted much of his time to works of charity and for the benefit of his fellow members of the Society of Friends. He was an early supporter of the Bible Society, and for many years the Society's Depot was in his premises in Union Street. G. R. published several small books and pamphlets, one an account of his son Isaac Richardson, who died in the Isle of Wight, soon after reaching manhood. Isaac Richardson was a most conscientious young man and was exemplary in all the relations of life. He took a warm interest in the Temperance cause, then beginning to claim attention. Some account of George Richardson and of sermons delivered by him was published by his daughter, Ellen Richardson, a few years ago.

Margaret Bragg was the widow of Hadwen Bragg, who founded the well known drapery establishment in Pilgrim Street. She resided at Summerhill, was a woman of ability and some force of character and was very stately in manner.

Daniel Oliver was a tea dealer and grocer, in the Bigg Market, residing there above his shop for many years until the business passed to his son. He was a very good man and in his later years was a picturesque figure in the streets of Newcastle.

Jonathan and Rachael Priestman lived at Summerhill, in a house adjoining that of Margaret Bragg and were well known throughout the Society. Their house was often the resting place of Ministers and others visiting Newcastle and not unfrequently large numbers of Newcastle Friends were there entertained. Rachel Priestman at a later period paid a long visit to the Meetings of Friends on the American continent, and during a still later visit to Friends in Ireland she was taken ill and died there. Jonathan Priestman was highly respected in Newcastle and was often placed in the chair at public meetings of a benevolent character.

The general appearance of the Meeting in those days was very different to what it is now. What used to be called the "plain dress" was worn almost without exception by both men and women, and the other peculiarities of the Society were more or less consistently maintained. Looking back there appears to have been more character and individual personality in the members than there is now, and some could express their sentiments with force and much frankness of manner. A few had come to Newcastle from the country districts of Cumberland and Allendale and were settled here in various trades and occupations. The Monthly Meetings were held then as now at Newcastle, Shields and Sunderland, but always in the morning at ten o'clock, those at Shields being more numerously attended by Newcastle Friends than when held at Sunderland. The journey to Shields was most frequently made by water. Wm. Hotham, a Friend in business on the Quayside and known to the boat owners, arranging for a good and clean vessel. After the business of the Meeting was over a walk to Tynemouth would sometime fill up the rest of the day. But at that time it was a not uncommon occurrence for a steamboat to stick fast on a sandbank. The first time the writer went to Shields the boat was detained an hour from that cause.

Visits to the Meeting by Ministers from a distance would then appear to have been more frequent than is the case now. I remember the visits of Richard Barrett, J. J. Gurney, Wm. Forster, Maria Fox, Benjamin Seebohm, Mary Nicholson, Isaac Sharp, J. B. Braithwaite, and many others. These visits were sometimes supplemented by a visit to each family composing the Meeting, a very arduous undertaking which seems now to have fallen into desuetude. John Pease was not unfrequently here from Darlington on the Sunday, as were likewise Jonathan and Hannah Backhouse. The Quarterly Meeting at Newcastle was then the Winter one, held on the first Tuesday in January, and occasionally would fall on New Years day.

The "Beacon Controversy" caused some disquiet and discussion among the Members, but so far as I recollect it did not result in any secessions. One Friend, Sarah Forster, a Minister, did resign her membership about that time, but it was unconnected with the "Beacon" movement. She joined the Baptist body, but continued during the rest of her life to hold much friendly intercourse with her old friends. Another resignation which caused much regret was that of Esther Stickney, a valued governess in the Priestman family.

About 1832, there was an Essay Society amongst the members, meetings being held occasionally at private houses. At these meetings original compositions both in prose and verse would be read and discussed, the papers being afterwards circulated amongst the members. Later on a few of those who had taken a prominent part at these Essay Meetings decided to publish an "Annual" under the title of the "Aurora Borealis," and this was carried out at the Christmas of 1832. Those taking the most prominent part in this publication were Joseph Watson, Harris Dickinson, Henry Richardson, Anthony Harris Smith, and William Doeg. They were assisted by contributions from Wm. and Mary Howitt, Bernard Barton, Wiffen, the translator of Tasso, and a few others, mostly Friends. The book financially was not a success, but its literary contents were perhaps equal to most of the Annuals of that time. Before the book saw the light of day, one of its promoters, Harris Dickinson, died, and the circumstance is feelingly alluded to in the preface. The book may still occasionally be met with on the break up of Friends' houses.

From time to time minor agencies sprang up with the view of promoting mental improvement amongst the young. One of these was a small society of young men, who wrote papers on subjects of their own choosing, and whose place of meeting was a room in Gilpin's Yard. Another was the Askesian Society, which promoted lectures by its members on scientific subjects and on Natural History. Professor Daniel Oliver, Professor G. S. Brady, Henry B. Brady, and Robert C. Clapham were in their younger days active members of this Society.

During the absence of Geo. Washington Walker as the companion of James Backhouse in his long visit to Australia and South Africa, his letters to Margaret Bragg giving detailed accounts of their travels were frequently read at the Meeting House on Sunday evenings. These letters were often very interesting, particularly those describing their travels in South Africa and their visits to the various Mission stations. They were engaged in this work a good many years, and George Walker, a member of Newcastle Meeting, never returned, but settled, I think, in Van Diemen's Land. It may be mentioned, the public readers of these letters were most frequently William Backhouse and Charles Ianson.

Before I went away to school, I remember attending a special meeting held to consider the propriety of establishing a Sabbath School for young children on the Meeting House premises. This was decided in the affirmative, and teachers were then and there nominated. Henry Richardson was the first superintendent for the morning school and John Richardson for that in the afternoon. The school has been continued ever since with the usual varying success of schools, but probably it was never so successful as at the present time. Some years afterwards a class for adults was formed, and is now a leading feature in the undertaking. Henry Richardson continued to act as superintendent for some years, when the state of his health compelled retirement. He continued, however, to act as secretary of the Peace Society, and for some years conducted with the assistance of his wife a small monthly periodical called the "Peace Advocate," and when this was discontinued, another small serial intended mainly to influence young children was undertaken. Henry Richardson sometimes wrote verse, and published a poem called "The Church and the Camp;" this also was in advocacy of Peace principles.

The Friends in Newcastle took a warm interest in the movement for the abolition of West Indian slavery, and subsequently in that for ending the apprenticeship system which succeeded to the state of slavery. Many public meetings were held in Newcastle, at which generally some Friends would be upon the platform and a considerable sprinkling in the body of the meeting. One great attraction at these meetings was often the eloquent voice of George Thompson, one of the finest speakers of the age, and whose home when visiting Newcastle was at Summerhill. If I remember rightly, the Friends taking the most prominent part in the anti-slavery agitation were George Richardson, Jonathan Priestman, Wm. Beaumont, and John Richardson. Referring to slavery in America, it is well known that a few Friends in Newcastle purchased from his American master the freedom of Frederick Douglas, raising the money among themselves and their friends. Those who carried out this purchase were Henry, Anna, and Ellen Richardson.

The movement for the repeal of the Corn Laws was well supported by the Friends, but being more of a political question, it did not awaken quite so much interest as that for the abolition of slavery. John Bright was frequently in Newcastle at the home of the Priestmans, and his eloquent voice was often heard in the town. I think Joseph Watson took some part in the Anti-Corn Law agitation.

Looking back to about 1830, the being much engaged in political discussion and in party politics seems to have been discountenanced by the general body of Friends. I believe a few of the younger men in Newcastle were members of the Northern Political Union, a body founded to promote Parliamentary Reform which was secured in 1832. In a lecture to the Friends of Manchester, Joseph John Gurney deprecated being engrossed in political action or being animated by the spirit of party.

The Sewing Meeting was commenced early in the century, and has been continued since to the great benefit of many of the poor. The meetings were held at private houses from six to nine p.m , and I remember that during

F

his residence in Newcastle Charles Reckitt would often attend and read out of some interesting book to the workers. The Soup Kitchen was well supported by many Friends, and a few took an active part in its practical working.

A Book Society was in existence from an early date in the century, and subsequently a second society was formed. These two societies were useful in promoting pleasant social intercourse amongst the members and sometimes interesting discussions on current literature. But gradually as books became cheaper and libraries more accessible, both of these book clubs were given up. Public entertainments and lectures were then much fewer than they have since become, there was consequently more time available for quiet reading, and some of our members had considerable acquaintance with English literature. It may just be mentioned that the society has furnished four successive secretaries to the Literary and Philosophical Society. Some of our members have been actively engaged in promoting the education of the poor, and the Girls' Jubilee School owed much for many years to the constant care and oversight of Ellen Richardson. About 1822, Ann Gauntley had a private school for the younger children of Friends, and at a later date our late friend Robert Foster had for a time a day school in the Schoolroom at the Manors.

There being no meeting held on Sunday evenings, left that time at liberty for some social intercourse, and the members would then frequently call upon each other. The town was then much smaller and distances not so great.

The tanning business seems to have been rather a favourite one, for there were in 1836 five firms of Friends thus engaged. These were Jonathan Priestman, in Low Friar Street; John & Edward Richardson, at the White Cross, in Newgate Street; William Beaumont, at the Darn Crook; Charles Ianson, at the top of the Postern; and John Burt, in Thornton Street (the last now covered by the Tyne

Theatre). It is difficult to account for so many out of a small body being thus occupied, unless it arose from the fact that leather is an eminently useful article, and does not readily lend itself to the freaks of fashion.

A good many of the other members were in business as shopkeepers, some living above their places of business. Let us follow a few to their homes. In the short distance from the Meeting House door to Bell's Court were three shops kept by Friends living on the premises, viz., those of James Gilpin, Charles Bragg, and William Holmes. Bragg's was then the first drapery establishment in the town, and James Gilpin was the first chemist and druggist. James and Sarah Gilpin were both overseers, very hospitable in their own house, and always kind to their fellow members, and indeed to everybody. As I recollect them, there were few worthier people in the town than James and Sarah Gilpin. It was in these premises, after the Gilpins' business was finally disposed of, that that curious old manuscript book was found containing cooking and medical recipes written by several generations of the Fairfax family. This book has since been reproduced in *fac-simile*. Charles Bragg was a very gentlemanly man, somewhat stately in manner, but kind and considerate in his dealings with others. This business was carried on for many years, and the shop was much frequented by county families. The house above the shop was occupied by some of the apprentices and assistants under the charge of a house-keeper. William Holmes was a grocer and tea dealer, but in a few years after 1836, the business was discontinued, and he then went to reside in Rye Hill. It may be mentioned, however, that William Holmes was for many years treasurer of the Mechanics' Institute.

Daniel Oliver's shop was in the Bigg Market, and at that time he lived above it, but later on his son, Daniel Oliver, jun., came to live in the house. William Sutton's shop was in Mosley Street, he living in the house above.

Sarah Rooke and her three daughters were then living in Dean Street, above the shop of Bragg & Rooke. William Hotham was at the eastern end of the Quay, and lived there for some years. As a boy, I was sometimes at the house, and remember how enjoyable was the sight of the ships and the stir and bustle of the Quayside. At that time, vessels would be three and four deep along the whole length of the Quay, and there were many curious ships of Dutch build. William Watson and Thomas Tessimond were also in business on the Quay. Anthony Smith had a grocer's shop in the Side, near the bottom of Dean Street, living in the house above. On the opposite side, were the shops of Robert Wilson, John Hewitson, and Joshua Watson, and at the head of the Side that of Christopher Robinson. None of these latter lived above their shops. Jonathan Drewry had a grocer's shop on the Sandhill, not far from the bridge end. Henry Richardson occupied the shop in Union Street, formerly that of his father, who now lived in Albion Street. George Brumell lived at the north end of the town in Claremont Place, and his son in Eldon Street; Mary Morton and her daughter in Ridley Place; and Elizabeth Brady and her daughter in Oxford Street. The Ormstons occupied the large house in Saville Row, so long afterwards their home. I have some recollection of Robert Ormston the elder; he used to come to my father's shop, and was remarkable for the quickness and accuracy with which for so old a man he could reckon up the full price of his purchase. As a little digression, it may be mentioned that his son, the late Robert Ormston, was the possessor of some letters of Oliver Cromwell to Sir Arthur Hazelrig, one written in the evening before the battle of Dunbar. Robert Ormston had these letters printed in pamphlet form for private circulation amongst his friends, and they are given in full in the 3rd edition of "Carlyle's Cromwell," with a brief narrative as to how they came into the possession of that family. It seems that a grandfather of Robert Ormston had been a steward for the Hazelrig family, and happening to be present when there was a great burning of letters and other papers going on at Nosely Hall, their seat, begged a few for his own keeping, and Carlyle characteristically adds, "All England is somewhat obliged to him."

Most of the Friends however seem to have lived at the west end of the town. In 1836, on the south side of Westgate Hill there were living, Wm. Backhouse, Chas. Ianson, Wm. Beaumont, George Goundry, and the two families at Summerhill, Margaret Bragg and Jonathan Priestman. In Summerhill Grove were John Richardson, Edward Richardson, Henry Richardson, and in Summerhill Terrace, Charles Bragg, and a little later, Joseph Watson. John Hewitson lived in Cumberland Row, as did likewise Robert Wilson. Deborah Richardson and her daughter, Ann Richardson, lived at Spring Gardens, a villa house surrounded by gardens on the Barrack Road. The site is now covered by manufacturing premises. Jonathan Drewry then lived in Westmorland Street, and Sarah Robinson in South Street, in a house now within the circuit of Stephenson's Works and used as offices. Many of these Friends and those living above their shops in the town would seek fresh air and exercise in the old Forth. There were a few Friends living in Gateshead, Joshua Watson at Bensham Grove, Wm. Watson in Claremont Place, Wm. Wigham Watson in Sedgwick Place, Henry Walker in Claremont Place, and Henry Brady in High Street. Henry Brady was a surgeon and had considerable practice in Newcastle as well as Gateshead. At a subsequent date Henry and Hannah Brady became leading Friends in the Meeting and much time and labour was bestowed by them to further its interests. The Rowntree family lived on the Windmill Hills in a house adjoining the Mill. Wm. Rowntree was a man of exceptional ability and had great conversational powers. The Claphams after leaving

Benwell Grove lived at Friars Goose in a house close to the Chemical Works.

Some of those whose names only have been mentioned above stand out in memory. John Richardson was an Overseer in the Meeting and was extremely kind to young men, some of whom he would often receive at his house on Sunday evenings.

Edward Richardson on attaining manhood was troubled with ill health and continued delicate for the rest of his life. This prevented him taking the active part in the Meeting he might otherwise have done. During a sea voyage, he with his sister Ann Richardson were wrecked on the coast of Norfolk and rescued by the lifeboat. His wife, Jane Richardson had much intellectual ability and was I believe a contributor to the "Aurora Borealis" under a nom de plume.

Joseph Watson early manifested a taste for literature which was maintained more or less through life. He contributed, I believe, to Tait's Magazine, then a well known serial published in Edinburgh. One of his ballads, the "Lambton Worm," is well known, and he occasionally wrote verse in the Newcastle dialect. He was one of the founders and first secretary of the Victoria Blind Asylum. He was a kind and worthy man in all the relations of life, and as a solicitor held a high place in the Town.

Ann Richardson has been mentioned as living with her mother at Spring Gardens. About 1858 she was married to Robert Foster, and henceforth both were united in much philanthropic work in the town, and in labours connected with Newcastle Meeting. The Ragged School owed much to their care, and many can remember the hours of pleasant social intercourse passed in their hospitable home.

Joseph Richardson was a brother of George Richardson, and did not come to reside in Newcastle until some years after 1836. He had been captain of a merchant ship and I believe his vessel had been lost. After middle life was past he came to John and Edward Richardson's office and continued to be employed there for the rest of his life. He was for some time a Superintendent of the Sunday School, and to use a homely phrase, everybody liked him.

Thomas Potts was employed at Priestman's Glue Factory, and lived near the works at the " Crooked Billet." He had become a Friend by convincement and sometimes spoke a few thoughtful words in the afternoon meeting. He was comparatively an uneducated man. It was to Thomas Potts' cottage at Elswick that in the early days of the Sabbath school the children were once or twice brought on Race Wednesday afternoon. There were no facilities in those days for a distant excursion, nor was there during the races any closing of shops in the town. The walk by way of Elswick lane and then through the fields to the mound now forming part of the cemetery, and afterwards tea at Elswick, was probably as much enjoyed as many a more ambitious programme.

It has been mentioned that in former days there were generally a few of the sons of Friends living at the Braggs' house, in Pilgrim Street, and engaged in the shop either as apprentices or assistants. Of those that I have known, a few stand out in memory, Wm. Gray and Charles Reckitt would be there near together, though perhaps not actually contemporary, probably between 1838 and 1840. They were both long remembered for their amiable qualities and pleasant manners. Wm. Gray on leaving Newcastle was for a time in business as a draper in Glasgow, but was unsuccessful and for some years afterwards filled different positions both in the United States and in London. Ultimately he commenced the business of biscuit making and thus founded the house of Gray, Dunn & Co., one of the best known firms in Scotland. Charles Reckitt was always of slender physique and a few years after leaving Newcastle died of consumption. Two others recur to memory who were I believe contemporary at Bragg's, viz.:

Henry Tennant and Frederick Clark. Henry Tennant, whose name appended to Railway advertisements was afterwards so familiar at North Eastern Stations, came originally to the shop of Bragg & Rooke, in Dean Street, and on the closing of that business was transferred to the well known house in Pilgrim Street. He afterwards got an appointment in the Brandling Junction Railway, at Gateshead, and after some further changes became accountant to the North Eastern Railway Company, and ultimately General Manager, when he removed to York. He married a Newcastle Friend, Mary Jane Goundry. Frederick Clark after leaving Bragg's was in business for some years as a draper, in Gateshead, but afterwards went into the chemical trade. He married Phœbe Goundry, and was a useful and active member of Newcastle Meeting.

In 1836, and perhaps before that time, a young man fresh from a neighbouring colliery village, and who had himself worked as a boy in the pit, might have been observed regularly attending the Meetings of Friends and taking a part in the Sabbath School. Possessed of little school learning he laboured assiduously to remedy the defect, and with fair success. He was then employed in the tanyard of John and Edward Richardson, and continued there for many years. No one would at that time have predicted that he would ultimately establish a very useful and important agency in Newcastle for the management of house property and real estate, nor could in any degree have foreseen his future commercial success. Our friend, James Hindmarsh, has now (1898) retired from business and lives at Ryton.

For a good many years after 1836 those Friends who were householders or in business suffered a good deal from ecclesiastical exactions, as their predecessors had done before them for about two centuries. They declined to pay these claims, and their goods were accordingly seized, often to a much larger amount than the original claim. A

careful record was annually kept of these distraints. Before
Church rates were abolished, Friends would sometimes
attend Vestry meetings to oppose the imposition of a rate.

Of the names that have already been mentioned as
members of the congregation about 1836, the following
surnames have now (1898) disappeared from the list :—

Bragg.	Potts.	Burt.	Cutforth.
Priestman.	Tessimond.	Brumell.	Rowntres.
Oliver.	Smith.	Ormston.	Brady.
Pattinson.	Dickinson.	Morton.	Seckings.
Hewitson.	Fallows.	Gilpin.	Doeg.
Toward.	Wall.	Ianson.	Armstrong.
Brown.	Goundry.	Backhouse.	Anderson.
Donaldson.	Sutton.	Drewry.	Hotham.

In the period of time embraced in these notes, the
Society of Friends in Newcastle, as elsewhere, has under-
gone some change both in its aims and methods. A modern
English poet has written :—

> " Yet I doubt not through the Ages one increasing
> purpose runs ;
> And the thoughts of men are widen'd with the
> process of the suns."

Music, so long discouraged by former generations of
Friends, is now cultivated to a considerable extent, and has
added a new charm to family life. The technical terms,
" plainness of speech, behaviour, and apparel," have lost
their former significance, and peculiarity in these respects
has been generally abandoned. As the result of organised
effort, the Society is now engaged in Foreign Mission
work, and has Mission stations in Madagascar, Syria, India,
and China. This latter change is largely owing to the
efforts of our friend George Richardson. Both Foreign
and Home Missions have met with encouraging success
But viewed from the standpoint of 60 years ago, the
position of the Society was unique and well defined, and it
remained a quaint and picturesque survival of the great
Puritan age.

Missionary and Philanthropic Work.

In the days of George Fox it might almost be said of Friends as of the earliest disciples, that " they went everywhere preaching the word."

Not waiting till " after the persecution that arose," but in the face of the bitterest hostility they witnessed to their faithfulness by untiring travel and by stedfast endurance of fines, imprisonment, and even death.

This was followed by a period of comparative quietude of the body, though many were yet faithful, and active " in the cause of truth," and our local records shew how numerous were the visits of " travelling Ministers " to this town and neighbourhood in the days when such journeys were slow and tedious. During the fifty years from 1777 to 1827, we have a list of 120 visits, giving also the expenses of the journey by horse, gig or chaise to the next place, generally with a guide. The names of Esther Tuke, John Wigham, Sarah Grubb, John Pemberton, George Dilwyn, Sarah Stephenson, John Cruikshank, Mary Pease, Ann Tuke, David Sands, William Forster, Deborah Darby, Sarah Lyons, Stephen Grellett, Elizabeth Robson, Isaac Stephenson, Dykes Alexander, Robert Jowitt, Jonathan and Sarah Grubb, Nathan Hunt, Sylvanus and Samuel Fox, A. Dockwray, J. J. Gurney, and Jonathan and Hannah C. Backhouse, appear amongst many more, reminding us of Friends and families who have borne an important part in the Society's history.

Many of the Meetings visited, as stated in the paper referred to, are no longer given in the "Book of Meetings" of to-day. The inevitable drift from country to town has left many Meeting Houses empty, though a considerable descent from quaker ancestry often lingers in the district of extinct Meetings, retaining quaker predelictions.

A curios relic has been preserved which throws light upon these primitive times and the subsequent changes. It is a map of the six Northern Counties, prepared by James Backhouse, of Darlington, in 1773, and printed upon a large silk handkerchief for light carriage and easy reference when travelling. Whether worn as a wrap or in the pocket does not appear.

Then, as now, the county of Northumberland, North of Tyneside, is indicated as a waste wilderness, void of quaker life. Shotton, Lartington, and Yarm have no longer a place even among the "Small Meetings" of Durham; and Cumberland, Westmorland, Lancashire, and Yorkshire, abound with names which in our "Tabular Statements" have ceased to be.

The part which Newcastle Friends themselves have taken in itinerant ministry has been considerable at certain periods, but confined to a comparatively small number of members. The names of Ralph Bainbridge, George Richardson, Daniel Oliver, Jonathan and Rachel Priestman, appear to have been in these labours the most abundant: Ralph Bainbridge to Westmorland and Cumberland towards the end of last century; and, between the years 1808 and 1842, the "true yoke-fellows" next named undertook, jointly or severally, thirteen extensive journeys with certificates of the unity of their friends. They traversed almost every county of England as well as parts of Ireland, some repeatedly, having as companions in turn, when not travelling together: John Wigham, of Aberdeen; Solomon

Chapman, of Sunderland; Joseph Unthank, of Willington; Joseph Knight, and Caleb Wilson, of Sunderland; John Richardson, of Newcastle, or Thomas Robson, of Liverpool.

The name of George Washington Walker is interestingly mentioned in W. H. Robinson's " Recollections." This young man was engaged as assistant with Charles Bragg, when he felt it right to accompany James Backhouse of York in his missionary journeys in New South Wales, Van Diemen's Land, South Africa, and the Mauritius. He obtained the hearty concurrence of his friends, who furnished him with a certificate of their unity.

Geo. W. Walker was truly helpful to his colleague upon whom the chief service rested, as evidenced in the printed narrative of their ten years' travel.

James Backhouse returned the certificate in person in 1841, as endorsed on the parchment; he having left G. W. Walker in Hobart Town where he remained till his death in 1859 to water the seed they had sown together.

Rachel Priestman visited the Meetings in and around Philadelphia in 1843; and finally, accompanied by her husband, entered upon a course of visits to the Friends of Ireland, where she died after a short illness at Waterford in 1854. Her remains were interred at Jesmond Old Cemetery amidst a large concourse of mourners when the voice of her husband broke the solemn silence at the graveside with the words of Christian resignation; "The Lord gave and the Lord hath taken away! Blessed be the name of the Lord."

Since that time we find no record of any minister of Newcastle Meeting having undertaken gospel service away from home with "certificate of liberation" by the Monthly Meeting, though many journeys have been entered upon without such credentials.

There does not appear to have been much work done by Newcastle Friends prior to 1800 on the lines of the multitudinous philanthropies of the present day; and even of instrumental gospel ministry the congregation was destitute for some years before the close of last century. Nevertheless, during that period of quietism, the Spirit of God was moving and working powerfully in the hearts of some of His children, the fruit of which was afterwards clearly seen.

The efforts of Dr. Fothergill, of London, and his co-adjutors to rouse Friends to a sense of their responsibility in reference to the education of their offspring, led to the foundation of Ackworth School in 1779.

The interest thus awakened was widespread throughout the Society; and under his leadership, with many other kindred spirits like the Tukes of York, Friends acquired a name as foremost among the churches in the work of education.

Other Boarding Schools followed the lead of Ackworth in various parts of the country, till in 1841 Ayton School was established under the care of Durham Quarterly Meeting. Both these institutions have had the warm sympathy and help of Friends of Newcastle from time to time. The part taken by William Holmes will be mentioned later; and other local Friends continued to give much practical help in the management of these schools.

In local charities,—the Infirmary, established in 1751; the Dispensary in 1777; the local Bible Society in 1809; the Indigent Sick Society in 1820; the Aged Females' Society in 1835,—each in turn found hearty supporters among the Friends.

The efforts of Elizabeth Fry to reform the terrible condition of the prisons and prisoners in Newgate in 1813 stimulated Friends "in the provinces" to exert themselves for the amelioration of the inmates of their gaols.

Hadwen Bragg's letter of that year (already quoted) gives an interesting peep into our own Newgate, which stood at the foot of Gallowgate. It was addressed to

George Richardson and Daniel Oliver when on religious service at Leeds. He says,—

> "Dear Isabella Harris has had a meeting at South Shields with sailors and the wives, &c , of such: one at North Shields also, and one with the neighbours of Willington, held at the Mill: this last I attended on 3rd day (evening) It was a solid, favoured season to many; there appears to be a serious seeking class in that district. I thought Isabella was enabled to divide the Word in a clear instructive manner. Her mind has also been led to feel with the poor prisoners recently tried at our Assizes: and she is this morning (6th day) gone to sit with them in Newgate. My M B. (Margaret Bragg) came up with me yesterday from Shields after their week day meeting, and is with Isabella, accompanied by her son and cousin, A.C. A fear of numbers has restrained me from being with them.
>
> Since I. Harris and my M.B.'s return from their visit to the prisoners, I find that seven men were (attentive) and tendered; nine women who were sat with separately exhibited great hardness.
>
> Our dear friend, D. Sutton, feels much stripped and tried when you are all absent. He keeps nicely in health, and is often looking in at the workmen in the Meeting House. I hope he will be comforted in the finish at last.
>
> In dear love to you both, in which be pleased to unite my M.B. and daughter Rachel, (afterwards Priestman).
>
> I am very sincerely,
>
> Your Friend,
>
> HADWEN BRAGG.
>
> P.S.—Should opportunity occur please to present our love to cousins Robert and Rachel Jowett and Joseph and Sarah Tatham."

In later years, after the new gaol was built in Carliol Croft, systematic visits were paid to the inmates by lady Friends with the full sanction of the authorities.

The Anti-Slavery Society likewise found the heart of the North true to the cause of freedom; and for many years the time and energies of Friends and others were engaged in earnest advocacy until the passing of the Emancipation Act crowned their efforts with success in 1838.

In later times, the homes of Newcastle Friends often sheltered negro slaves· who had taken refuge in this country; and the marked personalities of Frederick Douglass, William Wells Brown, W. Box Brown, William Craft and others, were familiar in the streets of our town.

The story of the purchase of the freedom of two of these does not need to be repeated here.

The following record illustrates the readiness of Friends to act in their corporate capacity in aid of their fellow citizens as occasion required :—

> "It having been ascertained by abundant investigation that at the present juncture very great distress exists among the lower classes of the community, the following subscriptions are given to be applied in alleviation of this distress, whether that of the manufacturing districts through the medium of the London Committee of Friends, or that which has been ascertained to exist in Newcastle or Gateshead, at the option of the contributors under the care of the Committee appointed by Newcastle Preparative Meeting in the 11th Month last, viz: Jonathan Priestman, William Beaumont, George Richardson, and G. A. Brumell.—Newcastle, 12th Month, 25th, 1842."

Then follows a long list of Subscriptions amounting to over £131 " besides 65 yards of calico, a piece of cotton, 10 pair cotton sheets, and 340 two-pound cakes of bread."

The Soup Kitchen was another agency which, from its establishment, had the warm sympathy and active support of Friends. It was opened in the High Bridge; and the Rev. John Smith, Vicar of Newcastle, whose portrait adorns (?) the walls of St. Nicholas' Vestry, could be seen side by side with his neighbour George Richardson, with their aprons (not episcopal) serving soup to the hungry poor.

Few Members of our Society have taken seats in the Town Council of Newcastle.

The annexed paper may have its value as bearing upon the place which Friends might have taken in Municipal affairs had the legal requirements not deterred them, and the care that was exercised that they should remain true to their conscientious convictions :—

" FRIENDS WHEN CHOSEN TOWN COUNCILLORS.

At a MEETING of a COMMITTEE appointed by the SOCIETY OF FRIENDS of this Town, to examine such Provisions of the MUNICIPAL REFORM BILL, as concern the Members of the Society.

It was concluded, that no Member of the Society can consistently accept the Office of Alderman, Town Clerk, or Councillor, in any Borough.

For, although it appears that no legal Disability now attaches to the Members of our Society, in Reference to any of these Offices, yet in regard to the Office of a Justice of the Peace, and also to that of a Mayor, Alderman, Recorder, Bailiff, Town Clerk, or Councillor, or any Office of Magistracy or Place, Trust, or Employment, relating to the Government of any Municipal Corporation, the following Declaration is required to be made and subscribed upon Admission :—

'I, A. B., do solemnly and sincerely, in the Presence of God, profess, testify, and declare, upon the true Faith of a Christian, that I will never exercise any Power, Authority, or Influence, which I may possess by Virtue of the Office of   to injure or weaken the Protestant Church, as it is by Law established in ENGLAND, or to disturb the said Church, or the Bishops and Clergy of the said Church, in the Possession of any Rights or Privileges to which such Church, or the said Bishops and Clergy, are or may be by Law entitled.'

This Declaration was prescribed by the Statue 9 Geo. IV., cap. 17. and, though not set out, is expressly referred to and enforced by the 50th Section of the Municipal Corporation Act.

So long as this Declaration continues to be an indispensable Requisite, as it now is, it appears to this Committee to present both in its Form and in its Substance, an Obstacle to any FRIEND consistently acting as a Justice, or in any of the Municipal Offices before enumerated.

Signed,

GEORGE BRUMELL.
WILLIAM BEAUMONT.
JOHN RICHARDSON.
JOSEPH WATSON.

Newcastle, 12 Mo. 9th, 1835."

As already indicated, the cause of education has been warmly espoused by the Society of Friends. The establishment of the Jubilee School for Boys in the New Road, and more especially that for girls in Croft Street, was initiated largely by Friends, in lieu of public illumination, to celebrate the 50th year of the reign of George III.; and many will yet remember the part that Ellen Richardson and her committee continued to take in watching over this school for girls.

In 1847, the foundation of the Ragged and Industrial School found amongst its most earnest promoters and stedfast guardians several Friends, past and present, who have helped the efficient managers to work out its remarkable success.

The early pioneers in Temperance reform numbered a good proportion of members of the little congregation in Pilgrim Street, who by consistent example and public labour helped this movement amidst scorn and suspicion. Amusing anecdotes could be told of how some of those who afterwards became staunch supporters of this cause, at first regarded this unpopular reform.

The Peace Society's Committee met at the Meeting House for many years.

The minutes of 1843 mention the names of Edward Richardson (Treasurer), John Richardson, Daniel Oliver, W. H. Robinson, Richard Hoskin; also George Brumell, Jonathan Priestman, George Richardson and their sons, in association with Matthew Forster, Errington Ridley, W. B. Leighton, George Charlton and other earnest citizens.

As stated in our earlier pages the zeal of Friends of the 17th century in aggressive missionary effort, gave place in the 18th to a reactionary quietude; and it was not until the latter half of the present century that the duty of Friends towards the heathen ABROAD was at all fully realised. As the revival was largely due to the efforts of George Richardson it should not pass unnoticed here.

G

When his own age and infirmity precluded him from foreign travel he used the powers that remained to him. In his 86th and 87th years he wrote no fewer than a hundred autograph letters to Friends in various parts of the country, earnestly calling upon them to take this question up as incumbent upon every section of the Christian Church, and thus the conscience of the Society was aroused until in 1867 the first Missionaries were sent out by the " Friends' Foreign Mission Association." The work then begun has grown year by year till the expenditure last year amounted to £24,621.

The numerous departments of the work may be thus indicated :—

"1898 was the first year of the united operation of the F.F.M.A. with the Friends' Syrian Mission. Although the expenditure was unprecedently heavy, the income received, including contributions for Indian Orphans (£919) and the result of the special appeal at the last Annual Meeting (£5,000) was larger than ever before. At the same time, owing to repeated deficiencies of income, the work has been necessarily curtailed, and new and increased contributions are earnestly asked for.

In INDIA the famine has left its mark upon the district where our Friends are working. 1,684 adherents of the Mission are reported at the end of 1898, slightly less than last year, but three times as many as three years ago. 2,136 children attend the Sunday Schools, and 1,776 the Day Schools. The Medical and Industrial agencies, Zenana visiting, and itinerant preaching have been steadily pursued. There are now 750 children in the Orphanages, the cost of whose maintenance is £4 per annum for each child ; special contributions for this object will be gratefully received.

The MADAGASCAR Mission has continued its work under the French regime. The 180 congregations in the district need constant oversight. The number of scholars is increasing in the 201 country Schools ; 17,281 names are enrolled in these, and 850 attend the two High Schools at Antananarivo. The Medical Mission and Printing Press give important assistance to the work.

The Mission in SYRIA has been steadily maintained in all its departments. The Medical Mission is about to open a new centre at Abadiyeh. The Hospital during 1898 has been fuller than ever before. The Training Homes for boys and girls continue full. The village Schools have over 900 scholars, and the other gospel agencies at Brumana, Ras-el-Metn, and the out-stations have been actively prosecuted.

The political condition of CHINA in 1898 has affected our missionary work. Owing to the rebellion in the province of Sz-Chuan, our missionaries have had to leave the station at Sae-Hung-Hsien for a time. In Chung-King the work of evangelism, Schools, and Medical Dispensaries has been maintained, but under considerable difficulty.

In CEYLON the two missionaries at Matale have continued their work. They greatly need additional helpers."

The Sabbath Schools.

(Contributed by Herbert W. Edmundson.)

The building of rooms for these Schools in 1834 marked a new departure in local aggressive work among Friends. The following contribution from the present Secretary must be quoted *in extenso*:—

The Newcastle-on-Tyne Friends' First Day School was begun in the year 1834.

From an interesting letter, written to George Richardson by his wife, we learn that two Friends, Henry and Anna Richardson, had been for some time considering whether it would be suitable to have such a school under the management of Friends. In the early part of 1834, these Friends consulted with others, and met with much sympathy and many promises of support.

Leave was given by the Preparative Meeting to use "the large room" for the purpose of holding a School for Boys and Girls on First-days. A Committe of Friends was then formed, and this Committee issued a prospectus, the following extracts from which show the intentions of the promoters of the School :—

> " On looking around us we find ourselves placed in the midst of a mass of ignorance and moral wretchedness which the most vigorous attempts of Christian philanthropy have been unable fully to disperse.
>
> We see our fellow Christians of almost every denomination endeavouring to fulfil the second great Commandment of our Saviour, love to our neighbour, in those intervals of the Sabbath in which they cannot be publicly engaged in proving their respect to the first, love to our Maker ; and we cannot any longer remain idle spectators of their arduous labours.
>
> The advantage of superior information is undoubtedly one of those precious talents for which we shall one day be called to account ; ought we not then deeply to consider whether we are not wrapping it in a napkin and hiding it in the earth.
>
> The object in view is to read and understand the Scriptures, and by the interrogatory system to impress on their memories their sacred contents."

The Committee drew up rules for the management of the School, appointed teachers, and arranged a canvass for scholars.

The School opened on the 4th of 5th month, 1834, with 44 scholars and 24 teachers ; it was held at nine o'clock in the morning and two o'clock in the afternoon.

The first report states that the teachers, regular and occasional, had increased to 30 and the scholars to 100. This made it necessary to refuse admission to boys for some time. Besides the Scriptural teaching given in the School, elementary lectures on scientific subjects were delivered on week day evenings and were largely attended, and a library was begun with 320 books. The children were encouraged to get Bibles of their own, and in the first year 21 of them were supplied with 13 Bibles and 10 Testaments.

In the report for 1836 we find it stated that several young persons of both sexes, 14 years and upwards, had entered the School " unable to read a single sentence— thus absolutely shut out from one of the greatest privileges of a Protestant country, free and private access to the Holy Scriptures."

This report also mentions the trouble experienced with some unruly boys—trouble which was only increased by putting the offenders out—for we read of dirty water being thrown into the School, and of bricks and stones being rolled along the floor. So the conclusion was come to that "patience and kindly expostulation," as the report says, "were likely to be better remedies," and soon a great improvement is recorded.

The first entry in the minute book of Teachers' Meetings is one which is often repeated ; it urges teachers to impress upon their classes the importance of attending a place of worship.

Two years after the School began, a Temperance Association was formed to discourage spirit drinking, but the following year this was changed to a Total Abstinence Society, of which 33 scholars and 24 teachers became members. We hear of this branch of work again in the report for 1871, under the name of a Band of Hope ; four years later it became a "Juvenile Temple" connected with the Good Templars, and in 1891 a Band of Hope was again started.

The first School tea party was held in 1837, and in the same year we read for the first time of a magic lantern being shown to the children.

The summer excursion in Race Week was an early institution, and for many years Jonathan Priestman's field at Elswick was a favourite place for the outing.

The School was at a very low ebb in 1853, in consequence of the cholera epidemic which was then raging in the city ; but owing largely to the diligent visiting done by a retired teacher the School was subsequently brought up to something like its former size.

The senior class for young men was begun in 1857. It met in the Preparative Meeting House apart from the rest of the School ; the object being to impart instruction of a more advanced character than was adapted to the School at large. The first month of 1868 witnessed the opening of the " new " senior classrooms.

Singing was introduced into the School in 1871, and in 1874 a hymn book, specially prepared for the use of the School, was printed to the extent of 1,000 copies.

At the end of the year 1875, the Morning School for juveniles had become so small in numbers that it was resolved to discontinue it. Henceforward the Morning School was known as the Adult School and the Afternoon as the Junior School. In later years, however, there has been a tendency for them to lose their distinctive features in this respect.

Between the years 1874 and 1897 there are no striking incidents in the history of the School.

A Foreign Mission Fund was begun in 1885 to support a native teacher at one of the Friends' Mission Association stations, but it does not seem to have been maintained for very long. A similar fund was established in 1895, with the object of supporting an orphan girl in the Friends' Orphanage at Hoshangabad, India, at a cost of about £5 per annum. The monthly collections, however, were soon found to be large enough to allow of the School adopting a boy as well as a girl, both of whom it continues to support up to the present time.

The Manors Literary Society was begun in 1886 in connection with the School, and flourished for many years.

Consequent upon the steady and continuous growth in the attendance of scholars, the annual meeting of the Newcastle Friends' Home Mission Association, in 1897, carefully considered the urgent appeal for an enlarged Main School and better classrooms. (*See pages* 29-31.)

The re-opening was celebrated by special meetings held in the morning, afternoon, and evening of 31st of 10th month, several Friends from other meetings being present

More than 600 scholars and Friends gathered on the
Monday evening following, when the event was further
celebrated by a tea, followed by addresses delivered in both
Meeting Houses which were crowded. That these improvements were justified was proved by the very large increase
in attendance which immediately followed. This was the
great event of 1897, but the report also records the
inauguration of a branch of the Young People's Society of
Christian Endeavour. An Institute for young men, open
for two evenings during the week, was also begun, and
a Football Club was established, all three of these agencies
being still in active work.

Two extracts from reports of the School may be quoted
in conclusion as illustrating the spirit in which the work
has been conducted :—

"When we realise how plenteous is the harvest, though
the labourers are few, we cannot but feel that though the
responsibility of Sunday School teaching may be large, the
responsibility of leaving it alone is greater still, and that weak
though our attempts may be, if they are carried out in a proper
spirit, if we endeavour to continue firm and steadfast, under
the Divine blessing our labours will not be in vain.

We would desire gratefully to acknowledge the measure of
success which seems hitherto to have attended our efforts, and
we trust that patiently continuing in the work—patiently and
prayerfully waiting for the aid of Him, without whom we
can do nothing—that aid will be vouchsafed to us, and our
endeavours will tend to His glory and the advancement of His
Kingdom on earth."

The effect of the Adult School as a nursery and feeder
of the congregation has been a marked feature of the past
15 or 20 years, and has been the means of introducing a
number of new members into the Society.

"The Newcastle Friends' Home Mission Association,"
which was established in 1862, has done much good work
in various ways, especially in the maintenance of mothers'
meetings and benefit clubs—removed from the counter-
acting influences of the public house—of Bands of Hope,

and evangelistic meetings. The first of these was held in a
room in Silver Street for a few years, under discouraging
and adverse circumstances. Owing to smallpox in the
same building, it was removed to the A Class Room in the
Manors premises, where it was continued with but little
life until taken up by the men of the Adult School and their
teachers, who have zealously continued their efforts with
much more hopeful results.

Mission meetings of a similar character have been
conducted at various periods during the course of years in
Hamond Street and in the " Eldon Rooms " in lower Pilgrim
Street, as well as in the Victoria Street Club Room.

The Conditions of Social Life.

Contributed by Thomas Pumphrey.

A GLANCE at the accompanying map of Newcastle shews how strongly it contrasts with the present conditions of our City life.

Then the quiet Borough was snugly self-contained within its walls with large open spaces, crofts and gardens, and with purling "burns" flowing down the "denes"; when oil lamps and candles served to make the darkness visible; when the river and the "pants" furnished the only water supply for those who were not privileged with private pumps; when the business premises were also the usual residences of tradesmen; when dinner at noon and tea at four were the order of the day; when the navigation of the river was impeded by shoals on which the barges grounded at low water; and the banks of the Tyne were picturesquely wooded, and when * " Leafy June," instead of riding under "bare poles," spread her sails at Jarrow as gaily as at † " Paradise"; when the long row of windmills was a familiar feature on the horizon line, and the old Tyne Bridge, with its Tower and houses, was the one thoroughfare between North and South :—*then* life went along much more leisurely; men and women were more disposed to contemplation : manners and customs were more simple and unconventional than in these days of express trains, constant postal deliveries, telegrams and telephones, all indicative of the rush and hurry of the present time.

It is not difficult to see that these external conditions, even when modified by the changes of a hundred years, must have affected the life of our predecessors in the faith.

---

* See the Tyne and its Tributaries.   † A hamlet west of Elswick.

They lived much apart from general society ; their association even with their fellow Christians of other names was mainly limited to matters connected with the philanthropies of the day ; books were comparatively few and costly, and letters were like angels' visits—very far between—large quarto sheets, closely written and often crossed, took time to write and required leisure to read. An extract from one such to George Richardson from his wife may be read with interest :—

"Newcastle 6th of 8th mo., 1809.

My dear G. R.

Glad I am you are once more set afloat as thou terms it : how anxious, daily and hourly anxious, on thy account have I been, believing you were much tired. You have had close work, 57 family sittings and four meetings in 31 days, it was no wonder thou should be off thy appetite, for which cause I am concerned.

*　　*　　*　　*　　*　　*　　*

I wrote thus much before Meeting, and have been taking tea at our dear friend, D. Oliver's, who, with his Mary, desire their love.

We had last 5th day here a severe thunderstorm. My brother and his bride, W. R. and his bride with their attendants, were at our friend D. Suttons's taking tea returning the Bride's visits, and had just done when it began to rain very heavy. M. Sutton desired her husband to go upstairs to shut down the window in their chamber. D. S. was within two yards of the window when a fire ball entered and directed its course across their bed, seized the bell wire, rent their bed post, in short, it went nearly all through the house, it broke all the glass in one window, 4 panes in another, 3 in another, and 2 panes in another window, tore up several boards in the floor where the wire took its course, and tore away the ceiling in the staircase in several places rent the book-case from top to bottom in the parlour. M. Sutton was sitting getting her tea after the others had done, and it overthrew the coffee-biggin, broke two saucers and one coffee cup, and much more too tedious to mention. The young folks were some of them much alarmed ; R. R. so much so as to faint away. Dear D. Sutton appears thankful for his narrow escape, but if he had been taken I apprehend he is readier than most. I wish all were as well prepared.

*　　*　　*　　* ELEANOR RICHARDSON."

It was an age of plain living, when but little served
the majority for family maintenance : business was the
more easily held in subordination, though doubtless there
were not a few whose affections were well-rooted in
temporal things. Shops were sometimes closed for mid-
week meetings for worship, so that master and assistants
were free to attend them together. As most Friends lived
within a ten minutes' radius from the meeting house, both
the morning and afternoon congregations on first days were
well attended. The evenings were frequently spent in
social or religious intercourse at the houses of some who
kept almost an open door for such as inclined to accept a
general invitation.

The afternoon meetings, especially to those who had
been to the Sabbath School immediately preceding, were
necessarily drowsy occasions, when weariness of the flesh
militated against the life of the spirit. They were generally
longer in point of time than now, and were more often
spent in silence.

When Travelling Ministers requested a " Public Meeting " at short notice, the young men of the congregation
were employed to distribute the invitations during the
afternoon. These Sabbath occupations after a hard week's
work recal a playful reproof administed by a senior to a
junior Friend, whom he met with the bills in his hand, in
the words—

> " Six days shalt thou labour and do all that thou art able,
> And on the seventh thou shalt holystone the deck and polish
> the cable."

Much tract distribution was also undertaken by the
younger members during the leisure of the First-days.

The Meetings for Discipline were important occasions
in those primitive days, and notwithstanding the difficulties
of travel, were more numerously attended than in these
days of rapid locomotion. The following

Notes by John Foster Spence

graphically describe these occasions :—

" In the year 1828 Friends travelled from Newcastle
to North Shields and from Shields to Newcastle to attend
Monthly Meetings,—those from North Shields either by the
omnibus which left an Inn called " Greys," at the point
where " Coach Lane " joins the Newcastle turnpike, near
what is now Charles James Spence's house, or by " Shields
gig " from the Bull-ring. It is a pity one of the latter was
not placed in the British Museum! It had a method of
expansion peculiarly its own, and I have many a time
ridden in one with twelve passengers and the driver : the
poor horse was sorely put to it ; but, at the half-way house
at top of Willington Bank, both horse, Mr. Wascoe the
driver, (an extraordinary man, afterwards an Alderman of
Tynemouth), and many of the passengers refreshed
themselves with home-brewed beer ! The omnibus was
considered the more aristocratic mode of conveyance, holding six inside and two by the driver: old William and
Margaret Richardson, Henry and Mary Richardson, the
Unthanks, Browns, and Spences competing for the seats.
As all could not be accommodated those who were
disappointed used to retire to the Shields gigs, or take a
steamboat at the New Quay. This was before the days of
the River Commission ! and the voyage was frequently of
a perilous and exciting description. Friends naturally
wished to be up in time for breakfast before the first meeting, and it was very tantalizing to be seated on a sandbank
for an hour or two, waiting for the tide to rise and float us
to the desired haven where a warm welcome was accorded
to the travellers, who, having started at half-past six or
seven o'clock in the morning, were quite ready to partake
of the hospitality of their friends. Often as many as
twenty or thirty Friends would be so received, many
returning to dine. This was the day of plum-coloured
coats and vests, drab kerseymere knee-breeches and top
boots or shoes with silver buckles, and hats after the manner
of the man who figures on the " Quaker Oats " bills : but

Friends wore a silk cord over the top to keep the brim
steady at the sides! The omnibus and gig drivers condescended to land you near the house you wished to reach;
and often has the writer been asked—"Are you going to
Gilpin's or George's or Daniel's?"

Sunderland Friends coming to Shields Monthly Meeting
had to cross the river in a flat-bottomed boat which was the
common receptacle of horses, carts, bullocks, and sheep, and
this sorely tried the spotless purity of Women-Friends'
fawn- or dove-coloured gowns and shawls. All Friends
kept open house on Monthly Meeting days; and very
pleasant were the afternoons spent after the more serious
business of Meetings for Worship and Discipline were over
and a good dinner had been partaken of. The younger
part of the community would retire to Cullercoats Cave
and there enjoy (surreptitiously) some of the good old
songs of the day,—Scotch, English, and Irish! I say
"surreptitiously" because it was considered wrong to sing,
and was very seriously discouraged. All this was long
before the days of railways. The Newcastle and North
Shields Railway was opened ten years later, and this
quicker mode of travelling soon revolutionized the old
primitive ways."

Quarterly Meetings were held in turn at Durham,
Darlington, Stockton, and Newcastle in the early part of
this century. A letter, subjoined, from John Richardson to
a Friend at Plymouth gives a lively description of one of
these great occasions, and helps us to realize the perils and
adventures incident to the maintenance of the Society's
discipline in those days:—

> "Spring Gardens, Newcastle-on-Tyne,
> 7th of 7th Month, 1825.
>
> "1 will now turn to give thee some account of our Quarterly
> Meeting excursion in which we have abundantly proved the
> diversities of travelling. About 35 friends embarked on board
> the "Britannia" of two engines of 25 horse each, on second day
> morning at ¼ before eight, reached Shields at ¼ before 9,

where 17 friends joined us, and Sunderland Pier at ¼ past 10, where 14 more made up the company. A fine, warm, westerly breeze, smooth sea, and smile on every face rendered the voyage delightful. We formed into social groups, or noticed the progress by the land objects, or pointed out the ships scattered about us, or paced the deck as inclination led us.

At the mouth of the Tees we took in Wm. Aldam and family for a short time, who are Friends from Leeds staying at Seaton, and who gave about a dozen urchins or sea-hedgehogs amongst us which they had been fishing for. As the tide had not risen sufficiently high we sauntered at the mouth of the Tees some hours, where a group of seals and a variety of sea birds interested us. We reached Stockton Quay a little after 6.

On third day night the wind had removed to the North-east, yet so little of it that friends embarked at ½ past eight on fourth day morning, without the slightest apprehension. We sailed finely down the Tees about 13 miles, but as we approached the sea the pilot, we took in, a little excited our fears by telling us he must go on to the Tyne as he could not re-land with his small boat on the coast for the breakers. As we got out to sea one after another fell sick. We stood against the wind, which was quite contrary, for some hours; the day was cold accompanied with small rain, which rendered it uncomfortable, yet only 3 or 4 of those quite knocked up went down to the cabin, of which poor brother Edward was one. In attending to him and getting him to bed, I fell sick, yet chose to lay on the deck. At last the captain not choosing to run risk of anything giving way with such a valuable cargo on board, put back to Hartlepool, where we were all safely landed. The next consideration, after an unrelished cup of tea, was to get homewards. Wm. Aldam kindly sent his carriage with some, besides which there were 6 fish carts engaged for the "sick, the women, children and baggage." After doing what we could to provide for our female friends, brother and I set off to walk, and reached Sunderland at ½ past 9 last night, 23 miles— thinking walking most likely to relieve our sickness, which indeed we found was the case. There were other companies of walkers, but as we set off between the carts, expecting they would overtake us, did not fall in with them. We left Sunderland at 5 this morning. Charles Bragg and I to Newcastle and my brother to Tynemouth. The "Britannia" is still lying weather bound at Hartlepool. The account of this curious journey has taken up so much room that I cannot give much detail of our Quarterly Meeting. It occasioned in this short journey a greater mixture of pleasure and profit, as well as of toil or trouble than I ever met with, though I think upon the whole the novelty of riding in fish carts gave a kind of social enjoyment that was not disagreeable.

At the Q.M. Isaac Stephenson gave a short account of his journey which was interesting, and produced from several friends expressions of gratitude to his Divine Preserver and Guide. He said he had never experienced such peace as since his return this time."

In literary and intellectual culture there have been Friends who have held leading positions. For many years one or both Secretaries to the Literary and Philosophical Society have been Friends; and some of our members have been foremost in promoting the establishment and success of the College of Physical Science. The Literary and Scientific Societies of 1853-1860 are graphically described by an abler pen; and "the Book Society" also deserves a special paper. The meetings of this union were amongst the pleasant social features of that period. These agencies certainly tended not only to stimulate the intellectual life of the Society, but were helpful in keeping alive and bright the good fellowship which is such a valued heritage.

Book Society.

Contributed by Alfred Holmes.

In considering the social conditions in the early part of this century, it is interesting to note what an important feature the "Book Society" formed in the social life of the times. There have been several Book Societies in Newcastle, but probably one of the oldest and one which had the longest life was that begun by a small body of Friends on April 27th, 1826. The announcement of its commencement was set forth in the following prospectus, which is interesting as showing the attitude of mind towards public libraries, very different from the freedom of the present day.

The Society of Friends are not more generally distinguished by their religious peculiarities than for their general character for intelligence.

It has long been a desideratum with the best informed and most enlightened members of our Society, to encourage the acquisition of useful knowledge, and utterly to preclude that of a decidedly hurtful tendency.

To propitiate so desirable an object, "Book Societies" have been established in many large towns. under such regulations as to ensure a strict observance of this very important and primary object.

Public Libraries are objectionable, inasmuch, as every subscriber may have free access to books of an injurious tendency, and that the youth may thereby acquire a desultory habit and fastidious taste, than which there is not a more prejudicial bias can possibly be given to the studious or recreative reader. But these objections are obviated, or at least very considerably lessened, by "Book Societies," into which no work can find admittance, the character of which is not previously known.

Independent of these considerations, important and great as they undoubtedly are, there are others which though less obtrusive, are not the less important or the less conducive to its general utility.

The frequent meetings consequent to its institution will necessarily create that peculiar feeling of fraternal regard, incident upon reciprocated interests, which, whilst it obviously tends to propitiate individual friendships, cannot fail to consolidate an unanimity in that which most intimately concerns us, the members of the same household of faith.

Something of this kind has long been wanting in Newcastle, and the projectors of this scheme confidently anticipate a favourable result, with the impression that its more early adoption can only be attributed to the absence of all definite propositions which, however, they now submit to the consideration of their friends with confident anticipations of the most favourable results.

The proposal met at first with little encouragement from some of the older Friends. Grave fears were entertained lest the new Society should be the means of

introducing unprofitable books into families, and it needed
not a little zeal on the part of its promoters to overcome
the obstacles which arose. Confidence, however, in the
motives of those who wished to establish the Society
prevailed, and knowing that nothing of an injurious
tendency was contemplated, twelve Friends came forward
and enrolled their names as the first members, viz :—

Charles Bragg	John Richardson	James Eaton
Mary Bragg	Edward Richardson	Ritson Southall
William Beaumont	John Burt	George Abbott
Sarah Beaumont	Joshua Richardson	G. A. Brumell

The last survivor of these was John Burt, who died in
1882, having been a member of the Society 56 years.

The meetings were held at the houses of the members
about once a month; tea was provided, after which the
business was transacted.

In looking over the minutes it is evident that the
actual obtaining of books in those days was a matter of
some difficulty. It must be remembered the completion of
the railway connection between Newcastle and London did
not take place until June 18, 1844, or eighteen years after
the commencement of the Society. The practice of the
local bookseller was to issue a list of books which he had
for sale, from which the purchaser could select; if it were
necessary to order books which were not in the stock list,
it would sometimes be several months before the volumes
were delivered.

One of the first books proposed and rejected by the
members was "Atrocities of the Pirates," proposed by
Charles Bragg, who also was sufficiently broad minded to
propose Sir W. Scott's novels, which, however, were
described as "prose works" in 10 vols. This proposal was
rejected and a few years later a similar proposition met
with the same fate.

The first Secretary was George Attley Brumell, who
retained the position for six years.

H

An elaborate system of fines seems to have been rigorously enforced, until one member having kept a book 206 days beyond his allotted time, the fine amounted to more than double the cost of the volume; it was then decided that the maximum fine should be the value of the book plus 14 days @ 2d. per day. It is difficult to understand the reason of the latter stipulation, as apparently a more equitable arrangement would have been to deduct this. Fines are frequently remitted for non-attendance at meetings for sundry reasons which are generally specified in the minutes: on one occasion in 1829 John and Edward Richardson were excused as they were "engaged at a fire."

Great care was evidently exercised in the selection of the books, which were always sent in the first instance for the perusal of the proposer, who not unfrequently withdrew his proposal, paying the cost of the book.

A minute in 1832 read as follows :—

"Tait's Magazine ordered at our last has been received, as far as it has been published, but this meeting being of opinion that it is unfit for this Society it is ordered to be suppressed and for the future discontinued. This meeting further instructs the Secretary to send back to the publisher the numbers of Tait's Magazine already received, and to state to him in general terms the reasons which have induced the Society to take the step."

Possibly this communication may have had some effect upon the publishers, as a few years later the magazine was again taken into circulation.

One of the special features of the Society was the annual sale by auction of the books, which for many years was held at Summerhill, the hospitable home of Margaret Bragg, when the rule made at the beginning that no wine or refreshment should be offered after the meeting was relaxed, and Friends were regaled on leaving with cups of hot cloved elderberry syrup.

Meetings were occasionally held in summer time at Charles Bragg's at Lintz Green, friends attending being conveyed in brakes. One of the minutes respecting such a gathering reads as follows :—

"Three brakes were hired from George White (one was very severe travelling, so much so that in coming back some refused to ride and preferred to walk) at a cost of £3 15s. 0d., tolls 8/8, three drivers 2/6 each and 2/6 to Christopher — total cost £4 13s. 8d. 42 persons were conveyed and a charge of 2/6 each exacted which leaves a balance to the credit of the Society. The weather was fine and the meeting and its friends enjoyed themselves amazingly. No mishap or regret except the jolty conveyance."

That the meetings were not always so harmonious is evidenced by a minute about the same time which reads :—

"There was a piece of work about the Life of Sir John Richardson by Rev. John McIlwraith, and it is determined to bring it forward at another meeting."

* At one period the members becoming too numerous a Book Society was begun at Gateshead, the two Societies uniting for the sale of the books. This does not appear to have lasted for long, and a number of the Gateshead members ultimately rejoined the old Society.

The general cheapening of books, the extension of Libraries and the increasing opportunities for intellectual enlargement, gradually affected the membership of the Society, and in 1872 the discontinuance was discussed. A great effort was then made to revive it and the struggle was continued until 1884, when it was finally decided to allow the Society to gradually liquidate itself. The last meeting was held at James Richardson's, South Ashfield, on May 18, 1886, when the books were sold, and the assets of the Society, which then consisted of a ballot box, a box of peas, the auctioneer's hammer, and 2/- were presented to the Secretary and Depository.

The "Askesian" and "Literary Society."

Contributed by Elizabeth Spence Watson.

The younger members of the Society of Friends seem to have been full of mental activity and of industry half-a-century ago if we may judge from the records of the two Societies,—the "Askesian" and the "Scientific and Literary Society,"—formed respectively in 1858 and 1855.

The title was certainly an apt one; for Chemical, Meteorogical, Astronomical, Geological and other Sciences were the objects of research, and were discussed with ability and enthusiasm.

I well remember some of the lectures, which were given in the Low Meeting House, Pilgrim Street. The first lecture was on "Fixed Stars," and was given by James Richardson. The meeting was presided over by Joseph Watson. It was followed in this and subsequent sessions by,—to select just a few,—"Oxygen and its relations," by Daniel Oliver; "The Organs of Sense," by G. S. Brady; "Geology," by R. C. Clapham; "The Rebellion of 1745," by William L. Watson; "The Principal Forms of Attraction," by Henry B. Brady; "The Age of the Earth as deduced from Geology," by David Richardson; whilst talented outsiders, in the persons of Dr. Collingwood Bruce, Rev. James Snape, Dr. Embleton and Dr. Heath, also contributed lectures and added to the success of the Society. After having run its course successfully and pleasantly for rather more than five years it came to an abrupt end.

[ROBERT SPENCE WATSON adds "The Session of 1857-58, was the last which this Society held. In 1858, Daniel Oliver removed to London, where he rapidly attained a distinguished position as professor of Botany, and other active members left the town, and so reduced the strength

of the Society that those who remained did not feel equal
to the task of keeping it on foot."]

In 1855 the "Scientific and Literary Society" was
formed. This differed from the "Askesian" in that it met
at the houses of the respective readers of the papers instead
of at the Meeting House. The list of members includes
many well-known names:—Henry Tuke Mennell (who
then lived in the house afterwards converted into the Blyth
and Tyne Railway Station,) R. C. Clapham, John Dixon,
T. Whitwell, Jeremiah Head, David Richardson, Charles
Wilson Bragg, John Wigham Richardson, Robert Spence
Watson, besides two others not Friends, viz.: Diego Fallon,
a talented young Spaniard, and David Reid.

"The Relations between Employers and Employed,"
by David Richardson (occupying then as now a great
space among the problems of the time,) "Cottage and Villa
Architecture," by Charles Beale; "Causes of the French
Revolution," by H. T. Mennell; "The Theory of Sight,"
by C. Wilson Bragg; "Bessemer's Process," by John
Dixon; "The Poetry of Nature," by Raylton Dixon;
"Astrology," by J. Wigham Richardson; "Our Living
Authors," by R. Spence Watson; "On the Consumption
of Smoke" (still unconsumed alas! after more than forty
years,) by Edward Richardson, jun.; these are some of the
subjects taken from the list.

In reading through the minutes of this Society one is
especially struck with the full and admirable reports which
the zealous secretaries, Henry Tuke Mennell, followed by
Robert Spence Watson, gave of the lectures. Such
excellent resumés one does not often meet with in Minute
Books. Reports of the discussions following the lectures
are also given, and present a delightful view of the lively
interest taken by the members and their friends in many
phases of thought and action.

In August, 1859, R. S. Watson makes this pathetic
little entry in the Minute Book,—the last!

" Several meetings were held after this at Whitwell's, Watson's, Beale's, J. W. and D. Richardson's, but the 'Conversation Club' (the Society has just changed its name), will probably meet no more. Whitwell is in business at Stockton ; Beale has a berth at Leeds ; Head is going to be married ; Watson is studying in London ; and poor Wilson Bragg has departed, we trust and believe, to a better country. May we all join him there.".

[NOTE.—Thomas Whitwell died a hero's death in August, 1878, sacrificing his own life to that of his foreman. Charles Wilson Bragg was drowned in June, 1859, whilst bathing in the river Derwent at Lintz Ford, near to his own home.]

Biographical Notices.

REVERTING to the concluding words of the chapter descriptive of the Premises where the Friends of Newcastle have met for worship for two hundred years, we now attempt to present the characters of a few of the men and women of the past.

The material at command, covering the earlier century, has been extremely limited. We have given prominence to the narratives which have been gathered from unpublished manuscripts, and regret the necessity to curtail any of the contributions, most of which, as well as the portraits, have been most kindly provided by relatives of the deceased.

Our endeavour has been to collect memorials of a representative variety; and we fully acknowledge how many are necessarily omitted of others whose lives equally furnish lessons of instruction.

We recognize the danger of pourtraying too brightly the characters of departed friends, and are assured that their own life-story would have told that they had " done many things that they ought not to have done, and left undone many things that they ought to have done." The minutes of the meetings for discipline record too many grave moral delinquencies to be entirely passed over without mention here. It is plainly evident that many a worldly heart has beaten beneath the collarless coat. With this frank acknowledgement we gladly draw the veil, desiring to bear in mind our own infirmities so that we may strive to live under the power of that grace by which so many of those who have preceded us were enabled to overcome the temptations to which we all are incident.

Elizabeth Clapham—1792.

AMONGST the cloud of witnesses to the efficacy of Divine
Grace, and to the great importance of experiencing its
purifying operation in time of health may justly be
numbered the subject of the following memorial.

She was the daughter of Reginald and Elizabeth
Holmes and the wife of Anthony Clapham, of Silver Street,
Newcastle-on-Tyne. She died in the 12th mo., 1792, a
minister about two years.

Of the early part of the life of this our endeared friend,
but little has come to the knowledge of the writer of this
article ; except that under the invigorating influence of
strong filial affection, she was enabled with a pious solicitude
to watch over the declining years of her venerable parents,
during a long and tedious confinement She was of a
lively and cheerful natural disposition, and yielding to the
early visitations of redeeming love and power, she was
brought under the purifying influences of the Spirit of
Christ, and being taught of Him, her mind became richly
stored with heavenly wisdom, by which she was prepared
to stand forth as an advocate in a cause dignified with
immortality and crowned with Eternal life. It was not
only by her public appearances in the Ministry of the
Gospel, but she was also often engaged in private conversation for which she was well qualified, to endeavour to
turn the minds of those with whom she conversed to seek
after enduring substance ; in which labour of love she was
often favoured to make a useful impression, so that she
truly became as a " Mother in Israel."

Although she had only attained to middle age, her
health became precarious. On the evening of a First day
of the week, having been prevented getting to meeting
as usual, she remarked, that she had on some former
occasions when prevented by slight indisposition or other

causes felt uneasy as though she had on too slight ground suffered herself to neglect this important religious duty; but on this occasion she felt peaceful in staying away, believing that it was not required of her.

About three weeks before her death, as she sat with a few Friends in her own house she was led to desire an opportunity of solemn silence, when she addressed the company, remarking that she felt her own mind in a state comparable to that of a little child, needing very frequent supplies of spiritual food.

On the day of her decease, she appeared in her usual health and went to meeting. Near the close she was engaged in a short but lively testimony from the text " Righteousness exalteth a nation—but Sin is a reproach to any people." Soon after she had resumed her seat, she was observed by those near her to be sinking down, and on being borne out of the Meeting House she became extremely sick—saying " Surely this sickness is unto death." Being taken to an adjoining house, in a few minutes she requested those around her to be still, when she was engaged to pour forth the breathings of her pious soul in the following pathetic supplication: " O Lord! thou knowest that I love thee, thou art my chiefest joy, and to promote thy Truth is my greatest rejoicing; my whole life is devoted to serve thee; come life or death, O Lord, be merciful to my soul. Be thou the support of the faithful in this place, and preserve thine elect everywhere." Thus our beloved Friend, in life exemplary and in death instructive, passed after two hours of extreme pain, calmly out of this transitory state of existence, and we humbly trust is entered the regions of Eternal blessedness.

(From George Richardson's Memoranda.)

Ralph Bainbridge—1729-1793.

RALPH BAINBRIDGE was brought up amongst the lead mines and in his youth worked at that employment. He became a member and a preacher of the Society of Methodists but, becoming dissatisfied with some of their practices and with their doctrinal views, he joined the Society of Friends in 1752 and appeared in the Ministry about a year after, and finally settled in Gateshead near Newcastle. He did not travel extensively in the line of the Ministry, but I have a brief memorandum of two journeys before me. The first to the meetings in Cumberland and parts of Westmorland, in part of which he had the company of James Graham, then of Kirklington. He left home 11th of 11th mo., 1783, and returned on the 30th. The second was the year following, when he visited several meetings in Yorkshire, Lincolnshire, Cambridge, and Essex. His health began visibly to fail in the spring of 1793, and the last meeting he attended was 2nd mo., 24th that year.

Accompanied by my brother Isaac Richardson I visited him twice in his last illness. In an opportunity which we had with him on the 10th of the 3rd month, 1793, he expressed himself to the following purport. On being told that the doctor had said that he thought him better he replied " Yes, he told me he thought the fever abated and that he hoped to-morrow to see me better; but whatever he may think, I believe 1 am on the very brink of the grave." After a little pause he added " I have many a dull and weary hour by night and by day, but when I am a little easier so as to be able to recollect myself and to look around I see nothing more that I have either to do or to undo. 1 had a desire to make an alteration in my will which I put off some days, thinking I might get a little better so as to write it myself : but as I did not but grew weaker, yester-day I got it done; and seem now to have nothing more to do with the world. In a religious sense it is so too : I have looked over the Quarterly Meeting, the Monthly Meeting, as well as our own particular meeting and cannot see anything further for me to do as to the ministry. I have endeavoured to discharge my duty to my friends. I have no particular certain view respecting the time but I think I shall never meet my friends in a public meeting again. It seems as if the prospect of the Society or of a feeling of the state of things was quite taken from me : almost as if I had never known them, so that my work seems nearly finished. Though we hear and read of people at these times having great openings, sights and revelations, seeming enraptured with Christ's love and of His meeting them, it has not been so with me; but I have been in a quiet rest, a waiting state, a composure, feeling a coming of that which was my morning light : that which called and created me anew and placed me in a state of sonship. He is yet with me : and I know that where He is I shall be also. It is not likely that I can do it myself again : I could wish my friends to be informed that I rest in the same faith,—in that which gathered us to be a people : I feel Him to be yet with me ; the God which kept me and fed me all my life long : the Angel which redeemed me out of all distress."

Respecting the Ministry he said :—

"It has appeared to me as if our Society is in great danger of suffering from those who are not rightly called, running into many words in man's wisdom not attended with life. But much lies with those who are set as Watchmen on the Walls. Let them do their duty toward poor young ministers : encourage when it is needed ; and when an undue forwardness appears let them drop a word of caution in tenderness and honest simplicity. Let them who are called readily answer ' Here I am, ready to go at thy command ;' and so humbly wait to feel the Holy One with them. A few sentences dropped under His influence will have their use." At another time, speaking of his outward

affairs which he thought might be pretty easily wound up
he said :—" I have had many fair opportunities to extend
my business, and by closing in with the offers which have
presented, I might perhaps have had a few hundreds more
to leave behind me : but I had seen and been afraid of the
snares attending a large trade ; and have endeavoured for
sometime past to lessen rather than encrease it : the reflection of which now affords much satisfaction."

On the 31st of the 3rd mo., he expressed himself nearly
as follows ; after requesting that his dear love might be
presented to friends at the then approaching Quarterly
Meeting at Durham, he said :—

" I have for some days been thinking a good deal
about the Quarterly Meeting. Some things have been presented to my view which I have endeavoured to put by,
but they seem to remain with me. Though I have always
endeavoured to do my duty and seem clear on that account,
yet if it had pleased Divine wisdom to have permitted me
to sit with my friends in that meeting again I might have
had something further to communicate. Though much
labour has been bestowed on the Quarterly Meeting, there
has appeared to me something like a sucker sprung up as
from the root of the vine, and the life and sap goes with it.
It is of the wild olive nature, and may be compared to the
lawful things—the other lovers—which seem to suck and
draw away the sap of life which has been afforded to the
minds of divers who stand high in outward profession,
active members who sit in the seat of the Rabbi,
but who have not been faithful. They have been
ready to execute the Lord's commands so far as suited
their own wills and inclination, but they have kept
alive things which ought to have been slain, and it will
be said to them as it was to Saul ' the Kingdom
shall be rent from thee and given to a neighbour of thine
who is better than thou, who will fulfil all my will.' But
there are others who come in the littleness of self, esteem-

ing themselves the meanest in their Father's family : these I hope will be favoured with Divine regard, and strengthened to come forward in the Lord's work. Such are invited under a feeling of the Father's love, and have at seasons to use the inviting language,—' Come brother, let us go up to the mountain of the Lord, to the House of the God of Jacob.' It is pleasant to us all to have our strength renewed in sweet fellowship together. I believe there are several young men and young women—striplings—who are under the preparing hand, and who I hope will be strengthened to come forward. These, if faithful, may rise up and take the crowns from the heads of some of the Elders ; those who are esteemed in their own eyes, some of whom would at times be saying to others, ' follow us as we follow Christ ' : but they have not that life attending their words which only can draw and gather the minds of the people to the true Shepherd."

I well remember the patriarchal and prophetic manner of his delivery and the peculiar solemnity which accompanied it. He died on the 27th of 4th month, 1793, aged nearly 64 years. He was a man of a strong and vigorous mind, cheerful and instructive in conversation, as well as lively and powerful in ministry.

By the removal of Elizabeth Clapham and Ralph Bainbridge, the particular meeting of Newcastle was stripped of instrumental ministry ; but it is with me here to record as a testimony to the efficacy of Divine Grace and to the inward operations of the Holy Spirit, that at no time of my life have I known a greater growth in the root and life of true religion than in the few years which followed, and I have reason to believe that I was not alone in this experience.

(From George Richardson's Memoranda.)

ROBERT FOSTER meeting his grandson ROBERT FOSTER, late of the Quarries.

Robert Foster—1754-1827.

ROBERT FOSTER was the eldest child of Dodshon and Elizabeth Foster, of Lancaster, and was born the 24th of April, 1754.

He spent 7 or 8 years at the school of John Jenkinson, of Yealand Conyers, where he acquired a good English education and the rudiments of Classical knowledge. He afterwards went to the Free School at Sedbergh, where he boarded with James and Mary Burton, at The Hill, whose daughter Mary he subsequently married. When about 18 years old he went to sea, and after making three voyages with Capt. Roper, in the "Marquis of Rockingham" to the West Indies, his grandfather and great uncle, Myles and James Birket (who were West Indian merchants at Lancaster) appointed him their storekeeper in Antigua. In 1774, after paying a short visit to Lancaster, he went again with Capt. Roper for the last time to Antigua, as supercargo, and Thomas Backhouse, of West Lodge, Darlington, was the cabin boy.

It appears by Robert Foster's own Log-book that he entered on board the "Endeavour," a Government brig, carrying 14 guns, about the end of May, 1776. She was fitted out in Antigua, to cruise against American privateers. His friends did not hear of it till the 9th March, when James Birket writes as follows in his Diary : "There is an account in town from the West Indies that Robert Foster, my nephew, has entered on board a Man of War's Tender, as mate and midshipman, to the inexpressible grief and anxiety of his father, grandfather, relations and friends. Oh foolish boy! Farewell! every tender reflection and connection with his best friends."

He left "The Endeavour" at Spithead, in June, 1778, and went on board "The Defiance," 64 guns. He only remained in "The Defiance" till July, when he entered on

board "The Jupiter," 50 guns, as master's mate, Capt.
Reynolds commander. He was probably induced to make
this change from his father, grandfather, and great uncles,
being well known to Capt. Reynolds, they having been
amongst his most influential supporters in several contested
elections which he stood along with Sir George Warren for
the Borough of Lancaster.

Robert Foster writes in his Log-book, October 21,
1778, "The Jupiter" had a severe engagement with "The
Triton," 64 guns.

On the 21st April, 1779, he writes "Pelican," River
Tagus, Received Capt. Reynolds' acting orders, as
Lieutenant of this ship. The "Pelican" carried 24 guns.
In August, 1779, his brother Myles died at Ulverstone,
aged 20, and his sister Elizabeth, having heard that the
"Pelican" was at Portsmouth, wrote to her brother, urging
him to endeavour to obtain leave to visit his father. On
the 5th September, as her father and herself were on their
way to meeting, they met him. They immediately turned
back much affected, and his father retired to his room quite
overcome. He took off his sword and tossed it under a
book-case, where it remained during his stay. The following
First day he went to meeting in the uniform of a lieutenant
of a man of war; next day he returned to Portsmouth.

James Birket writes in his diary, November 3rd, 1779,
"Robert Foster came home this morning after a long
fighting campaigne in sundry Men of War. He quitted
the fighting trade at his grandfather's request, and seems to
be a very sensible youth."

R. F. was never disowned for his violation of Friends'
principles,—he was visited by sundry Friends appointed by
the Monthly Meeting, to whom his acknowledgments
appear to have been satisfactory, as no further notice seems
to have been taken of his case.

Not long after this R. F. turned his attention to
farming, and became tenant of Hebblethwaite Hall, near

Sedbergh, and the land attached to it, the property of his
grandfather, who gave him the stock and let him have the
Farm of 331 acres rent free. No one could know much
less about farming than he did, but he had the assistance of
an excellent bailiff. He was industrious and worked hard.
His style of living was much that of other north country
farmers; masters and servants taking their meals at the
same table in a room called "the house," a little superior to
the kitchen, but with a stone floor. A black fleece and a
white fleece from his own sheep, carded and spun by his
housekeeper and woven in the neighbourhood formed the
cloth (called self grey) for his working clothes. Amongst
his various acquirements he had gained some knowledge of
medicine and common law,—the first he made useful in
prescribing for the poor and the second in drawing out
Wills and settling the disputes of his neighbours. It was
once said of him that "Where mystery was to be
unravelled, confusion brought into order, or truth made
conspicuous, he was capable above most men." In 1783,
R. F's. great uncle, Jas. Birket died, leaving him the Wood
estate on Cartmell Fell, which had been in the family since
1679. In March, 1784, R. F. was married to Mary Burton,
who had been his housekeeper. In the spring of 1785,
R. F's. maternal grandfather, Myles Birket died, leaving
him both the Hebblethwaite Hall and Sarthwaite estates.
After the land become his own, he let it, retaining in his
own hands only sufficient for the keep of two cows and two
horses, besides the woods and plantations in which he took
great interest, planting thousands of trees, chiefly larch,
with his own hands. It was a saying of his, that "a larch
would buy a horse before an oak would buy a saddle."

There were some poor families in the neighbourhood
of Hebblethwaite, living an idle life, the children
uneducated and unemployed; with a view to raise their
condition, he built a small mill for spinning coarse woollen
yarn. This gave employment to some, and others at their

I

own houses by knitting the yarn into large stockings, such
as were worn by men engaged in the Greenland Fishery;
also into caps and gloves, etc. When a stock of these had
accumulated R. F. took a journey on horseback to
Newcastle, for the purpose of disposing of them. His first
call was on Wm. Spencer, Quayside, who, without giving
him time to speak said "I cannot attend to you, I am
engaged." R. F. bid him "Farewell" and was leaving
the shop, when he called him back and said "You are not
like other travellers, I see you take an answer when it is
given you, what have you got?" On seeing the samples
he asked the prices, and R. F. told Wm. Spencer that it
was his first journey on a business of which he was very
ignorant, and which he had entered upon mainly for giving
employment to some poor families. He then asked W. S's.
opinion as to prices and he not only gave him an order, but
mentioned some shops at Shields, where he might use his
name as an introduction. W. S. continued to be his best
customer. R. F. proceeded on horseback to North Shields,
where he arrived in drenching rain. In searching for an inn
at the Wooden Bridge, he lost his way, and continued
along the Low-street to the extreme end of the town.
Seeing a bridge at a distance he urged his horse through a
high tide to reach it and then found it to be the Low
Lights Bridge, far beyond the point he aimed at. He
asked a man if he knew any inn where he could put up his
horse and get something to eat. The man said he did not
think there was one, but seeing that R. F. was a Friend,
said "There's Mr. Taylor, one of your sort of people who
lives upon the bank, I daresay he will give you something
to eat, and I think they have a stable." R. F. then did
what was not known to have been done before—rode up
the Low Lights Stairs to *Henry Taylor's back door, told

* Henry Taylor was another fine old sailor, a friend of Capt.
Cook, and the projector of the two Lighthouses at Hasbro' Gatway,
which have been the means of saving much property and many
valuable lives.

him his adventures and said "being wet and hungry and
almost at my wits end what to do, I was advised to come
here, Wilt thou take pity on me?" Hy. Taylor said "Yes,
but thou had better go into the kitchen and get thy clothes
dried, and they will give thee something to eat." After a
while H. T. looked in upon him and said he was going out
to call on Bartlett Gurney, a friend from Norfolk then in
town on a visit. R. F. said "I know him." H. T. looking
at his rustic-clad visitor rejoined "Why, does thou know
Bartlett Gurney? He said "Yes, and I should like to see
him if thou has no objection to take me with thee." They
then went together and H. T. was much surprised to see
the cordial way in which B. G. received R. Foster and
introduced him to his relative John Walker, of Dockwray
Square. H. T. finding his visitor of a different class to
what from his dress he took him to be, invited him to stay
all night promising not to put him into the kitchen again.
This singular introduction was the origin of an intimacy
between them and their families which continued for many
years. In 1791. R. F. went up to London at the request
of William Wilberforce, to give evidence before a select
committee of the House of Commons on the Slave Trade in
the West Indies.

In 1796, he took into partnership Joseph Dover who
had been brought up in the woollen trade and greatly
extended his business, built another mill and manufactured
several kinds of coarse cloth: travelling into adjacent
counties, particularly into Cumberland, to see his purchases
of wool weighed and packed, he formed wide acquaintances
and made many friends. At this period R. F. took great
pleasure in botany and in teaching it to his children, often
taking some of them with him in his country rambles for
that purpose.

In the spring of 1799, his wife in returning with him
on horseback from Kendal Quarterly Meeting, was exposed
to wet, and took a severe cold which terminated in

consumption. She died the 9th November, 1799, aged 46. After this afflictive bereavement R. F's. sister Elizabeth went to live with him. She was a very superior woman, and her society was a great advantage to his daughters and a comfort to himself. She continued to be a frequent visitor to Hebblethwaite Hall after R. F's. second marriage in 1802, with Margaret Burton, the widow of John Burton, brother of his first wife.

The Poet, Wordsworth, spent a week at Hebblethwaite in 1804 or 1805. He gave R. F. a letter of introduction to Robert Southey ; and Coleridge was also an acquaintance. Another of his intimate Cumberland friends was John Fletcher of Greysouthern ; they corresponded in Latin.

In 1808 his daughters Elizabeth and Mary went on a visit to Newcastle, Shields and Sunderland, when friendships were formed which led eventually to the marriage of Elizabeth to Anthony Clapham of Newcastle (1809,) and of Mary to Robert Spence of North Shields (1810). At the time of the visit alluded to, R. F's. son James was serving his apprenticeship with Hadwen Bragg of Newcastle, and his son John with Procter and Spence of North Shields.

In June, 1812, R. F. had a severe attack of rheumatic gout. This appears to have decided him to sell his landed estates, which he carried into effect the same year. It was with great regret he parted with Hebblethwaite Hall : it had been a hundred years in the family, but the step seemed necessary to enable him to make a fair disposition of his property.

Early in November, 1812, Robert Foster, with his wife, and daughter Sarah, removed to a house in Northumberland Street, Newcastle, which he afterwards purchased. His son John, who had become a partner with Anthony Clapham in the soap making business, then went to reside with his father. During R. F's. residence in Newcastle he was a frequent attender of the Yearly Meeting in London, an additional inducement being to visit his son James, who had settled in the metropolis. He was accustomed to make these journeys by sea in a collier, sometimes taking his wife or daughter with him; he also went three or four times to Holland, his object being chiefly to obtain a more perfect knowledge of the Dutch language. He was a director of the Newcastle "Savings Bank," which he attended diligently while health permitted. In February, 1824, R. F. had a slight attack of paralysis, and a few weeks afterwards his wife had a stroke of the same character, but much more severe. Notwithstanding this however, she survived her husband eight years. R. F. also recovered from his slight attack, but his general health was shaken and gradually became more and more feeble. His last illness continued for many months and was attended at times with severe bodily suffering, which he bore with much patience. He departed this life the 15th June, 1827, in the 74th year of his age.

From a M.S. biography furnished by his great-grandson,
Robert Spence Watson.

David Sutton—1736-1829.

DAVID SUTTON was born at Scotby, near Carlisle, and resided with his parents until he was about twenty-five years of age; when he removed to Newcastle for improvement in the line of his business, that of a house carpenter, where he continued for a few months. During this period, he became acquainted with Rebecca Moor, to whom, a few years afterwards, he was united in marriage, and finally settled in Newcastle.

When he left the parental roof for Newcastle, his father accompanied him on foot a few miles. When they parted David became very thoughtful; and proceeding a little onward, he stopped by the way side, where he was

DAVID SUTTON.

led to supplicate the Lord, like the patriarch of old; beseeching that He would be with him whither he was going.

Being careful to walk in the fear of the Lord, he grew in religious experience and in favour with his brethren in Christian fellowship; and in the year 1773, he was appointed by the Monthly Meeting to the stations of overseer and elder; which important offices he continued usefully to fill, during the long period of fifty-six years: performing services incumbent upon those who occupy such stations until within the last month of his life, being favoured to retain his mental faculties, as well as his spiritual perception with extraordinary strength and clearness.

He gave up business about thirty-two years before his decease; but he was careful to guard against contracting habits of inactivity and indolence, which in some cases creep upon those who are similarly circumstanced. He spent much of his time in the exercise of gardening, which he believed contributed to the preservation of his mental as well as bodily vigour, and was almost daily engaged in kind and fatherly visits to his relations and friends, many of whom were often edified and instructed by his counsel and example.

He was diligent in his attendance of religious meetings for worship and discipline. In the maintenance of our discipline he was very useful, knowing its value well: and being of a weighty discerning spirit, he was a firm and upright pillar in the Church. When required to deal with delinquents, the meekness, tenderness and long-suffering which he evinced, united to much firmness and decision in support of our Christian testimonies, gained him the esteem and affection of many of those who found the narrow path which he recommended too strait for them to walk in. His manner of verbally answering the queries relative to the state of the Society in the Preparative

Meetings, in order that they might be committed to writing, was often peculiarly discriminating and instructive; and this talent continued with him up to the last year of his life. On one of these occasions, when about ninety years of age, in speaking of the diligent attendance of meetings on week days, he appealed to such as plead that they have not time to spare for this purpose in such a solemn and impressive manner as will be long remembered by those who heard him.

It was his frequent practice, on the approach of times of public excitement and temptation, to give an affectionate caution to his young Friends to beware of being drawn aside from the paths of virtue by giving way to the desire after vain sports or other improper indulgences. This he occasionally did at the close of a meeting for worship.

Although he was favoured to attain to so great an age, he was not exempt from occasional illness. The precious and heavenly sweetness that clothed his spirit and seasoned his conversation was instructive and edifying. He was enabled to sit through a Monthly Meeting till within a few weeks of his death.

In 1828 he penned the following memorandum:—
" Being now entered into the ninety-third year of my age, and lived to see six generations of my family, and to notice many turnings and overturnings that have taken place in that time, and now as the time of my departure is drawing near, perhaps I cannot do better than remind my dear grandchildren, and those that may read this memorandum, of the advice of the Royal Psalmist to his son who was to succeed him in the government :—' Solomon, my son, know thou the God of thy Fathers: serve him with a perfect heart, and with a willing mind: if thou seek him he will be found of thee, but if thou forsake him he will cast thee off for ever.'—(Signed) David Sutton."

In his last illness, he was confined to his house for about five weeks; and though at times his sufferings were great, yet he was serene and peaceful and at times cheerful, though quite sensible that his end was approaching ; his countenance beaming with love upon all around him. A while after, saying that he should soon be released, he fell into a gentle sleep and peacefully breathed his last.

Compiled from published Memoir with additions supplied by his great-grandson J. Wigham Richardson,

Isaac Richardson—1761-1810.
Deborah Richardson—1773-1848.

ISAAC RICHARDSON was born at Seghill, in 1761. His parents were John and Margaret Richardson : her maiden name was Stead. Seven years after their marriage they removed from the Seghill farm and planted the tan-yard at Low Lights.

At the age of twenty-three, Isaac Richardson entered upon the business of John Storey, tanner, of the White Cross, Newgate Street, in Newcastle, and being an industrious, successful tradesman he acquired considerable property : but as he grew in experience he became sensible of the insufficiency of worldly possessions without vital religion to promote true happiness either here or hereafter. His tastes led him to read many Reviews and other literature in which were mingled plausible insinuations which tended to undermine some of the essential doctrines of the Gospel. This predisposed his mind to give place to suggestions that were thrown out during the religious controversy which agitated the Society of Friends a hundred years ago. By the events which followed he was much weaned from such reading, and being humbled under the hand of God he became in degree more prepared to appreciate the attributes of our Divine Redeemer.

In the year 1795 he married Deborah, daughter of David and Rebecca Sutton, and resided for many years at

DEBORAH RICHARDSON.

Spring Gardens near Gallowgate. They had eight children, four of whom died when quite young. These sorrows, together with a heavy pecuniary loss by fire at the tan-yard and his own failing health were made the means of weaning him from earthly things.

Isaac Richardson was among the earliest members of the Lit. and Phil. Society. He interested himself in schemes for the education of the poor, reading a paper in 1806 on the propriety of introducing the mode of instruction proposed by Dr. Bell and Mr. Lancaster. His efforts in this direction afterwards bore good fruit.

He made several sea voyages for the benefit of his health: the last of these was to Plymouth, but growing considerably worse he returned, and just lived to reach the Wear where he was met by his near kindred and died peacefully on board the " Derwent " in the midst of them.

The day previous, realising his weakness, he said to his brother John that he was " not afraid to die, but felt resigned to the Divine will," adding that " all things in this world had greatly faded in his view," having been brought to trust only in the mercy of God for salvation.

He was fifty years old at the time of his death, leaving his young family and the business under the care of his brother George, who carried it on and administered the estate until his sons were able to relieve him. His widow survived him thirty-eight years. Their children, who lived to maturity, were John, Edward, Rebecca, and Ann who, later in life, married Robert Foster.

Contributed by their grand-daughter, Emma R. Pumphrey.

Rebecca Richardson.—1807-1834.

THEIR daughter Rebecca only lived to the age of 27. Two years before her death she writes: " Felt much

REBECCA RICHARDSON.

anxiety of mind to-day, having to act as clerk to the Preparative Meeting when the four queries had to be answered.
In thus endeavouring to lend a helping hand in the maintenance of the discipline of our Society, I do wish and even
pray that my willingness to perform this little service may
be blessed."

Her cousin Rachel Pumphrey (daughter of George
Richardson), writes from Ackworth in 1838, to Ann
Richardson in reference to Rebecca's death—speaking of
their stay at Cullercoats.—" How thoroughly I should have
enjoyed accompanying Ellen and thee in your sea-side

rambles. Ah! how this reminds me of days that are gone, when four of us joined in happy converse. One walk in particular seems so fresh in my recollection when our beloved departed one repeated Barbauld's beautiful hymn on those sands. I think I was never more struck with its beauty. . . . Almost four years have flown past since she was taken. May it be our chief endeavour to let the day's work keep pace with the day!"

Hadwen Bragg—1763-1820.
Margaret Bragg—1761-1840.

HADWEN BRAGG was born in Whitehaven in 1763. He was the son of John Bragg and his wife, Margaret, whose maiden name was Hadwen. Being placed as an apprentice with a respectable tradesman of his native town who was not a member of the Society of Friends, he was exposed to temptations tending to lead into some deviations from the principles of his religious profession. This occasioned him much thoughtfulness, and, as the termination of his apprenticeship drew near, he was increasingly concerned to seek after an acquaintance with that power graciously afforded to preserve the dependent mind in the path of safety. After the expiration of the term he spent a short time in London, where goodness and mercy continued to follow him. On his return to Whitehaven he had an advantageous offer of a share in the business of his former employer, which he thought it right to decline from a conscientious fear lest he should be led to deviate from a strict adherence to testimonies which, though some may esteem them of minor importance, he had seen it right for him to bear. This step was a close trial of his faith from the surprise which it occasioned to his kindly interested friends, and because at that time no other situation presented itself as a provision for a livelihood.

MARGARET BRAGG.

After accompanying two Friends on a religious engagement in Scotland he visited Newcastle-upon-Tyne as an entire stranger to the place, and in the year 1788 concluded to fix his residence there, and opened a drapery business in that town, at the corner of Mosley Street and Pilgrim Street. In the latter years of his life he was often led to look back with feelings of pious gratitude in contemplating that providential arm which, in his early years, had protected him and had guided him to this conclusion.

In 1790 he married Margaret, the youngest daughter of Isaac and Rachel Wilson of Kendal. They were fellow-travellers in the way to the Kingdom, and endeavouring to walk in the Divine counsel, they grew in religious experience and became prepared for usefulness in the Church. Their hearts and house were not only open to receive the Lord's messengers and servants, but they were enabled to extend a kind and fostering care towards those of less experience.

Early in the present century they removed from their house above the place of business to Summerhill, then quite in the country with a view of trees and corn-fields stretching to the river. The road to it lay through the West-gate and his friends thought it "was a lonely walk for Hadwen Bragg with the owls hooting at nightfall."

Hadwen Bragg was appointed by the Monthly Meeting to the station of Overseer at an early period of his life, and a few years later to that of Elder, both of which offices he filled with much usefulness to the time of his death. By his faithfulness and prudent zeal in the affairs of the Society, carefully following what he believed to be the pointings of the Spirit of Truth, he was made instrumental in promoting the firm, yet tender, exercise of the discipline of the Church.

He was also liberal in promoting works of charity and assisted in conducting several Institutions in Newcastle for the relief of distress, the instruction of the ignorant, and the spreading of the truths of Christianity.

After a protracted and suffering illness Hadwen Bragg died in 1820. Thus closed the earthly existence of one whose life was peculiarly marked by love to his fellow men and by a more than common interest in the peace and welfare of the religious Society of which he was a member.

Margaret Bragg survived her husband twenty years. She had derived much advantage from her pious training, and was, in early life, favoured with precious visitations of Divine love. She first spoke in the ministry in her thirty-fourth year, and, growing in her gift, became a diligent labourer. She visited at different times most of the meetings of Friends in Great Britain and Ireland, where her faithful and zealous labours of love proved a refreshing visitation to many. She was diligent in attending meetings, with a close, searching ministry; a tender visitor and sympathizer with the sick and afflicted, and a liberal contributor to the poor.

To the end of her life she continued the parental care which she and her husband had exercised over the young men and apprentices employed in the shop, and many other young Friends partook largely of her kindness and hospitality, it being her especial care to notice in this way the more friendless amongst them. She was endowed with a superior share of natural ability; and possessing a strong and active mind, whilst her family and domestic concerns claimed much of her time and attention, she was able to take part in the management of a variety of affairs beyond the generality of her sex.

Her last illness was short, during which she frequently breathed the language of prayer and thanksgiving. She died at Summerhill, aged seventy-nine years. A minister forty-five years.

(Contributed by the Family from published memoranda).

The following extract from a letter, written by Sarah (John) Richardson to her sister, Susan H. Balkwill, at Plymouth, gives a picturesque view of Margaret Bragg "at home":—

"William Beaumont took tea with us on first day. I do not think he has taken any share in the proceedings of the committee for getting up the "Aurora." I think it looks as though Charles Bragg had the Colliers still in view by sending the Prospectus to them I met him last evening at Summerhill, where we attended the Essay Meeting. I let him know that W. Collier thought favourably of the thing. We attended at a short notice with an essay of sister Rebecca's on "Fortitude." Sister Ann's a very good and pretty description of the neighbourhood of Keswick. Edward and Jane's two poems on the promised "Aurora"— Edward's much remarked upon as very *original* metre, or no metre at all but irregular verse. Some of the other subjects were on Contentment, on Prayer, on History, The Cholera, Friendship, Parting, The Grave, The Speedwell, The Holly Evergreen. A Magazine Ditty, by Joseph Watson, a very clever six-line verse on the events of the Past and the Coming Year. William Doeg's, a very long piece, good and clear, proving that great talents are not opposed to the possessor uniting amiable qualities, and that it is not merely to be affectionate that we can be amiable, &c., &c.

Margaret Bragg presides on these occasions—fancy her seated in her own corner, with a little round table and one candle, busy the whole evening knitting. Next her I sat, then Ellen, Isabella Watson, one of the Hewitsons, cos. George Richardson, William Gray, Henry Hotham, Hadwen Priestman, then a large round table, on it books, papers, and a basket of flowers. W. Doeg and J. Watson seated at it as the readers, then Margaret Priestman, sister Ann, E. Clapham junr., Elizabeth Priestman, Mary Clapham, sister Rebecca, Anthony Atkinson, Chas. Bragg, Esther Stickney, David Doeg, Harris Dickinson's sister; then near the door, on a couch, drawn a little forward towards the fire, Rachel Priestman, my John, and Jonathan Priestman. Thus, as well as I can, have I given thee an idea of the friends that sat round that spacious, well-appointed sitting-room, a glowing fire and a warm welcome making all look and feel comfortable.

4, Summerhill Grove,
24th of First month, 1832.

K

DANIEL OLIVER.

Daniel Oliver—1771-1848.

WAS the son of Andrew and Jane Oliver, of Benwell Hills. He had not the privilege of instruction at a Friends' School, and by association he was led into hurtful amusements, yet (as he wrote) " I felt the reproofs of instruction in my own breast." After leaving school he was employed for a time on his father's farm, and when about eighteen years old learnt the mercy and goodness of God. When he reached thirty-six years of age he felt constrained to open his mouth in public testimony. He entered into trade, where his conduct was marked by uprightness and circumspection.

He freely left his outward concerns to attend our meetings and to engage extensively in the service of the gospel. In 1842 he was deprived by death of his estimable wife (Mary Oliver) to whom he had been united for forty years. He retained his mental and bodily faculties until he had nearly completed his seventy-seventh year; and was able to attend meeting until about six weeks of his decease. He peacefully departed on the 2nd of 4th month 1848: a minister 41 years.

Joshua Watson—1772-1853.
Esther Watson—1786-1862.

JOSHUA WATSON, the son of Jacob and Hannah Watson, of Tedham in Allendale, was born on the 16th of eighth-month, 1772, and died at Bensham Grove, Gateshead, on the 11th of second month, 1853.

He belonged to one of the earliest of Northumbrian Quaker families, and was himself a good type of a North Country Friend, plain and direct of speech, resolute, a trifle irritable, and with his temper not always quite in control, no respecter of persons, one to whom the substance meant all, the form nothing. Allendale, the calf-yard of the Watsons and Wighams, has had many such men. When that courteous, kindly, but bashful gentleman, William Beaumont, shook hands with Cuthbert Wigham at Quarterly Meeting, he said, hospitably,—"Cuthbert, wilt thou come up at three o'clock and pick a bone with me?" "Na, na, Willum," was the reply, "if I wait till three o'clock I mun hae something better than a bone to pick." That was Allendale way: the direct, blunt, but perfectly genuine speech of the Norsemen and old English men who had stuck to Allendale and its vicinity.

Joshua Watson was a lead miner when a young man; and thus a member of a most democratic confraternity. Each man took his bit of ground to be explored at a certain

JOSHUA WATSON.

figure from the Lord of the Manor: there was not the relationship of master and servant. But the town had its fascination for him, and he came to Newcastle in 1803.

Three years after he married Esther Watson, daughter of Joseph and Rachael Watson, of the Riding, Allendale Town. She was fourteen years his junior, and she survived him nine years. She was a gentle, loving woman, of a quiet and retiring disposition, but calm and wise in counsel, much beloved by all who knew her, and she exercised a powerful restraining influence upon her somewhat impetuous and impulsive husband.

He lived in the Side,—then almost a fashionable quarter of Newcastle—over the shop in which he carried on the business of a cheesemonger. Behind this house and shop his garden ran up steeply to the Moot Hall. When his eldest son, Joseph, was born, in 1807, he was anxious that the child should have plenty of fresh milk; and, laying down the little garden, or garth, in grass, he bought a cow: but the problem was how to get it into the garden! A long and steep flight of stairs intervened between the Side and the garth. Joshua Watson was little of stature but a Hercules in strength, and he carried the astonished cow up the stairs and deposited it in the garden,—no doubt with much groaning of spirit on the part of both!

He was indeed a Hercules. In early youth he had thrown the champion wrestler of Cumberland; had leaped on to the head of a wild stag at bay in a rocky pool, and held it down until ropes were brought and it was led securely away. With old-fashioned gallantry, when acting as guide in his native parts to two lady Friends engaged in the ministry, he threw himself over an open pit-working and made for them a bridge of his body that they might pass over the narrow but perilous strait to the fair land beyond, otherwise inaccessible for them.

On his 78th birthday he crossed the High Level railway bridge from Gateshead to Newcastle, part of the way on a

ESTHER WATSON.

single plank; and was told, at the Newcastle side, by George Stephenson himself that he was the first man who had done this.

But I might go on multiplying tales of his original deeds for many pages : let me only say further how, under a stern and, to children, rather affrighting exterior, he had the gentlest and softest of hearts. A man of genuine and unaffected piety ;—" one who never turned his back, but marched breast forward,"—and whose whole life was a simple, honest endeavour to do his duty towards God and man as a faithful follower of Christ.

John Hewitson—1782-1855.
Jane Hewitson—1775-1870.

JOHN HEWITSON was born at Ellershope, Allendale, the 17th of third mo., 1782. He was educated at such schools as the country afforded, which were of a very poor class, the teachers for the most part being very unfit to perform the duties they had undertaken.

He often spoke of being visited by the tendering influences of his Heavenly Father's love at a very early age, and as he grew older, though outward circumstances were unfavourable to the exercise of religious feeling, few of his associates being at all likely to be helpful to him in things which concerned his eternal happiness, yet his Heavenly Father did not leave him without a witness for Himself, which was, much to his regret in after life, too often set aside.

John Hewitson was a member of the Church of England, and in 1809 he married Jane Watson (sister of Joshua Watson), who was a member of the Society of Friends. She was disowned in consequence. He frequently

JANE HEWITSON.

JOHN HEWITSON.

felt an increasing desire after religious knowledge, and used often to say that he believed his acquaintance with her was of divine ordering and proved very helpful to him. About three years after their marriage he was received into membership of the Society of Friends, his wife also being reinstated. He had much to endure in taking up the cross which he considered it his duty to do, both as regarded dress and address, also in keeping on his hat in courts of justice. Using the plain language to his mother was a great trial to him, as it was considered disrespectful by his brothers and sisters (his father had died before this time), but he was enabled to keep to the pointings of duty; his mother made no remark, and thus the difficulty was removed. In 1815 they removed to Newcastle, and for several years he assisted his brother-in-law Joshua Watson in the provision trade; his income was small, but his wife was a careful helpmate, and they were enabled to live comfortably and in contentment, occupying a house in Pandon Bank, near Sallyport Gate. In 1821 John Hewitson commenced business on his own account, and so fearful was he of getting wrong that for a while he took stock once a month. The Almighty, who knows the secrets of all hearts, was pleased to prosper him in his endeavours after an honest livelihood. He was a diligent attender of meetings, and it is said frequently closed his shop door on a 4th day morning to enable him to do so.

They had two daughters and one son. About the year 1853 the whole family removed from Newcastle to Leeds to live with their son William Watson Hewitson, who had attained considerable eminence as an engineer in that town. John Hewitson died 4th of twelfth mo., 1855, and his widow in 1870 at the age of 95 years.

Jane Hewitson, daughter of Jacob and Hannah Watson, of Tedham, Allendale, born 27/4/1775, died at Headingley, Leeds, 6/5/1870.

William Watson Hewitson—1814-1863.

SON of John and Jane Hewitson, was born at Allendale 28/8/1814, and removed with his parents to Newcastle in 1815.

After receiving what was then considered a first-class education at Ackworth School and subsequently at a private school at Kendal, W. W. H. was taken into his father's business, but it was soon found that his talents lay in quite another direction, for in spare moments he was always drawing models of parts of machinery, locomotives, &c. His father was, however, wishful that his son should succeed him, and it was only after it became evident that he would not make a tradesman, that he gave his consent in 1829 to his being apprenticed to Stephenson & Co., mechanical engineers, to go through all the grades, beginning at the very bottom. (This business was only commenced in 1824). Here he found exactly the field which he desired for his talents, and after a service of some seven years, during which time his mechanical genius was rapidly developing, he removed in 1836 to Leeds.

His first engagement was with Messrs. Todd, Kitson and Laird as a draughtsman, and here his ability and energy were so marked that only seven years later he was taken into partnership. At that period of rapid railway development the firm of Kitson, Thompson and Hewitson was in the front rank in locomotive construction, and W. W. Hewitson's early history is a fine object-lesson to many a lad whose position in life depends on his own exertions.

During the twenty-seven years he resided in Leeds he won the esteem of many by his executive ability and kindness of heart. As an instance of this thoughtfulness for others it may be mentioned that when Asiatic cholera was prevalent in Leeds, and seventy of his firm's men were down with it, he visited all of them at their homes at the

WILLIAM WATSON HEWITSON.

risk of his own life ; and his cheerful temperament and wise suggestions as to treatment went a long way towards the restoration of many of them.

W. W. Hewitson was connected with several other important industries besides the locomotive works. A warm attachment existed between John Fowler, the inventor of the steam plough, and himself, their characters being very similar, and it would have been difficult to find two men at that time who did as much for the prosperity of the town and yet were so little in evidence.

In the year 1852 W. W. Hewitson bought the Woodlands at Headingley, and here his love of science was indulged in the acquisition of the latest inventions in microscopes, lamps, electrical appliances, &c., and among others a curious clock, said to be one of the six made by the inventor.

He died on the 14/5/1863 in his forty-ninth year, and was interred in the Friends' Burial Ground, Camp Lane Court, Leeds, the funeral being attended by a large number of his fellow-townsmen and the employés of the firm.

John Richardson—1799-1859.
Sarah Richardson—1802-1889.

THE tendency of the religious teaching of the Society of Friends, under Divine guidance in everything, is towards self reliance of character, active and industrious habits, and simple tastes ; John Richardson exemplified all these. He was the son of Isaac and Deborah Richardson, of Newcastle, and was educated first at Bruce's School, and was afterwards for some time under the care of Joseph Sams of Darlington—a great student and traveller of his day. Of a family who for generations had been in the tanning trade, John Richardson served an apprenticeship with his uncle John, at his tanyard in Bishopwearmouth, and on coming of age entered the business established by his father Isaac Richardson, in Newgate Street, Newcastle, and continued it with his brother Edward until death severed their close and brotherly partnership. They often combined with their business journeys the attendance of Yearly and Quarterly Meetings, travelling by coach or by sea, and took part in important meetings in London in the causes of the Abolition of slavery, of International peace, of Free trade, the Anti corn law agitation, and the first meetings of the United Kingdom Alliance in Manchester.

The annual return of the whale and seal fishing ships to Hull, or to Peterhead, Fraserburgh, and Dundee often took one or other of the brothers into Scotland, necessitating large purchases. It is noteworthy that in consequence of the utilization of petroleums instead of whale and seal oils, for the first time this century no ship has this year, 1899, left Great Britain to continue this trade.

J. R. was always fond of gardening and the cultivation of vines. A mulberry tree in Summerhill Grove—probably the only one now within the City of Newcastle—is of his planting. Many drives to visit the gardens and hot-houses of country gentlemen, to inspect the bark of newly felled timber, or to and from a country house which he built in the valley of the Derwent, are remembered by his children with lively delight.

In the Society of Friends he filled the office of Overseer and Elder, being appointed to the latter station at the age of twenty-seven, and in many ways he served this section of the christian church in which he had been born.

On returning home from a journey with his wife shortly after his marriage, he found the furniture of their dining room had been seized and taken away because he would neither serve in the militia nor pay for a substitute.

His private memoranda clearly shew his endeavour to keep in check the love of the things of this world and his desire to train up his family in the fear of the Lord. A large hearted hospitality made his home the frequent meeting place for friends and for social and religious gatherings.

As one of the largest shareholders in the Northumberland and Durham District Banking Company, its collapse in the dark days of 1857 involved him in the loss of much of his property. No law for limiting liability was then in existence. The anxiety entailed by this disaster was grievous. Though a principal shareholder he had never had anything to do with the management of the Bank, or had he more knowledge of its financial condition previous to its stoppage than was made public. Nothing could then be done to avert the ruin and distress which its failure caused. For himself he humbly accepted the trial as a discipline and bore it with christian fortitude. He often expressed his consolation at having brought up his family in a way which rendered it needless to make any great alteration in their manner or style of living. More than a year of suspense during the liquidation of the bank's affairs told upon his health. The sale of his house and other property during this time of commercial depression was a most trying ordeal, but after settling with the liquidators of the insolvent bank in the spring of 1859, he went with his son James to Westmoreland, on a visit for rest and change of scene, and when walking on the road between Shap and Kendal, one very stormy day, he was seized with an attack of apoplexy which proved fatal. Carried into a lonely wayside inn, "The Plough," he passed away from earthly trouble, having just completed the sixtieth year of his age.

Sarah Richardson.

SARAH RICHARDSON was the daughter of Benjamin and Elizabeth Balkwill, of Plymouth.

When seven years of age she was sent to a Friends' School at Wellington, in Somersetshire, and remembered being taken out of bed while there to see the great comet of 1811. A day school for the children of Friends and others having been opened in Plymouth, she was afterwards sent to it.

During the war with France, ships might often be seen from Plymouth hovering on the horizon, and she could remember running home in terror as the cry was raised " the French are coming." She saw Napoleon Buonaparte on board the "Bellerophon" in the Sound, a captive after the battle of Waterloo; and long years afterwards happened to be walking on the Hoe when the troop-ship signalled her arrival from the Cape, having on board the body of the young son of Napoleon III., slain in Zululand.

The farmhouses in South Devon belonging to her relatives, were places kept in fond remembrance. These with their primitive ways, their apple orchards and cider presses, their dairies and clotted cream afforded data for many a tale, strong in contrast with the ways of the North Country to which her marriage transplanted her when twenty-three years of age.

Elizabeth Fry was visiting Plymouth, on one of her many errands of mercy at the time of J. and S. R's. marriage; she was present, and preached on the occasion, appending her name to the certificate.

To bring his bride home, John Richardson bought a four-wheeled conveyance with a hood. In this they drove from Devonshire to Northumberland, in 10th month, 1825, performing their honeymoon journey in three weeks.

Sarah Richardson devoted her best energies to the well-being of her large family. She possessed a remarkable gift in her power of graphic description of scene or character, for which the circumstances of her life afforded ample scope. The vividness with which the events of her girlhood and early married life were related, to those who sat beside her in later years, was very striking. She often recurred to her mistakes and failures in the management of her household. Sometimes a chapter of vexations, mortifications, or perplexities would be recounted with much pathos or humour, or the sore bereavements would be dwelt upon which had been allotted her in the loss of four children in their infancy and two sons in maturer years. The recital of these and many other touching memories generally concluded with a fervent thanksgiving unto God for his abounding mercies.

She survived the crushing troubles of 1858-59 for thirty years. Her widowhood was passed in the same house in Summerhill Grove, to which she originally came in 1825.

The following Lines were written by one of her sons on the occasion of her death :

> Dear mother, as the solemn hour draws nigh
> When we must take our last farewell of thee,
> What crowding memories come floating by ;
> And in them all with grateful hearts we see
>   Thy tender care.
>
> Thy loving hands in childhood's helpless hours,
> Thy gentle voice so sure to bring relief,
> To guide our steps and strew the path with flowers ;
> But weary limbs, and tears of pain and grief
>   How oft thy share.
>
> The old home feels the hand of Death at last,
> For us thy gentle heart has ceased to beat,
> But feebleness of age for thee is past ;
> And loved ones—parted long, now join to greet
>   Life's peaceful close.
>
> Dear mother, in our hearts thy name we keep,
> Sweet memories of thee to our latest breath,
> And grief is softened as we watch thy sleep
> And see upon thy much loved face in death
>   Such calm repose.

JAMES GILPIN—1788-1855.
Son of Benjamin Gilpin of Manchester.
Born at Manchester.   Married Sarah Spence.

SARAH GILPIN—1793-1863.
Daughter of Robert Spence of Hartwith,
Knaresbro' Forest.

WILLIAM HOLMES.

William Holmes—1792-1858.

WILLIAM HOLMES was born at Sunderland 16th Jany., 1792; he removed to Newcastle about 1820, married Ann Smales of Whitby, 18 Dec., 1822, and died 11 Jany., 1858. Though not his business he had a natural talent for planning, and acted as architect for the erection of many buildings. Amongst others he designed and superintended the erection of the Schoolrooms on the Meeting House premises, with the warehouse and buildings in the Manors.

These were built in 1833 at a cost of £2,060, the amount being raised by loans from six Friends, W. Holmes

being one, and the £300 still owing to the Preparative
Meeting, the loans being gradually repaid with 4% interest
out of the rents of the Meeting House property, and finally,
liquidated Dec., 1851, except an annuity agreed to be paid
to a Friend for £100 sunk, which remained two years
longer.

W. Holmes was the acting member of the Property
Committee in charge of the Pilgrim Street premises for 13
years, till 1843, when Robt. Wilson took charge for 17
years, till 1860. Wm. Henry Holmes acted for 35 years,
till 1895, when it was transferred to the present Committee.

The following extract from the history of Ayton
School by George Dixon gives further proof of his capacity
in this department of practical work for others.

"I find the following minute of the Ayton School Committee
dated 7th month 27th, 1841 :—

"The Building Committee report that the proposed alterations are in a state of progress, the estimated cost of which is
calculated at short of £500; the oven and steam apparatus
included.

" William Holmes of Newcastle made the plans and superintended the alterations and erections from the commencement
to their completion. He took down two old cottages and all
the buildings between the gable end of the old house and what
is now the Boarding-house, and erected a three storey building,
which remains the same to this day. The upper room was
intended for a dormitory for the boys, the middle room for the
girls' school-room and dining-room, and the room on the
ground floor for the boys' school-room.

" He restored the passage way leading from the village to
the kitchen behind, and the stairs, for access to the rooms
above, and the upper storey of the old house, which was to be
the girls' dormitory In the kitchen he fitted up a steam
apparatus for ovens and cooking.

" The food was sent up by an elevator to the dining-room,
by which the empty vessels were returned to be washed.
Great credit is due to William Holmes for his ingenuity and
economy. His mind seemed to be occupied by the alterations
both night and day. About two o'clock one morning I heard a
knocking against the wall which separated our lodging from

the one adjoining : I felt greatly alarmed ; sprang from my bed and went into the next room, where I found William Holmes : he apologised for having disturbed me, and said :—' I wanted to know whether this partition was a brick wall or a stoothing ! ' On account of the large amount of old material which could be appropriated in the new buildings it was hardly possible to have the work done by contract ; hence every man was employed by the day. This gave William Holmes so much anxiety that he took board and lodging in the village for his wife and family to enable him more comfortably to superintend the work. Daily visits were also paid by Thomas Richardson, who had left Stamford Hill, London, on account of his wife's health, and was living at Ayton House, which he leased. In a letter to John Pease, Thomas Richardson expresses great satisfaction with the manner in which William Holmes was pushing forward the new buildings, and the great obligation the Committee was under to him for his unremunerated attention."

George Richardson.—1773-1862.

WAS born at Low Lights, North Shields, where his father, having removed from a farm at Seghill, had established a tannery—a business in which his grandfather had been engaged at Whitby, and his great grandfather at Ayton, in Cleveland.

In 1800 George Richardson married Eleanor, daughter of Joshua Watson, grocer, with whom he had served his apprenticeship in the Groat Market, Newcastle. In the same year he commenced business as a grocer in the Old Flesh Market, where they resided for many years, and made a home for their assistants.

Allusion has been made in previous chapters to his frequent ministerial journeys. On these occasions the cares of the family and the business were left to his wife, whose letters bespeak much anxiety in relation to both the children and the trade.

The extensive acquaintance which he made with Friends up and down the country made their home in

GEORGE RICHARDSON.

Newcastle the frequent resting place for these on their visits to Newcastle.

His published auto-biography, aptly entitled "A Basket of Fragments for Hungry Souls," sufficiently describes the subject matter of his ministry.

Though in his own particular meeting he was often silent, the reverence and fervency of his spirit betokened a mind stayed upon God, and the unction which accompanied his ministry left a deep impression upon those who heard him. In prayer, especially, he seemed to get 'within the veil,' while his soul was poured forth in fervent supplication for those assembled.

His interest in the Friends in Norway was long continued and earnest. From a small company of prisoners of war, who were led (before they had any knowledge of Friends) to sit in silent waiting upon the Lord on board their prison-ship at Chatham, and who were thus brought to the notice of Friends there and in London, they became, by persistent faithfulness in the maintenance of their conscientious convictions "a separated people."

They were supplied with Bibles and books in their own language, and were repeatedly visited by Friends after they were established as a Meeting at Stavanger, and were further fostered by correspondence and other proofs of sympathy until they increased in numbers and received accessions to their membership from the national church.

To escape persecution many of them emigrated to Iowa and other parts of the United States. This led George Richardson, in 1842, to write an earnest appeal "to those in authority in Norway" on their behalf. A copy of this document was handed by William Allen to the Swedish Ambassador in London for presentation to the King of Sweden. This was followed three years later by a resolution of the Storthing, which received the royal assent, and was issued with the signature of "Oscar" as an "Act of Toleration," granting to the Friends under his dominion "free public exercise of religion, separate registration of marriages, births, and deaths, exemption from taxes to the State church and its officers, other than tithes;" "the acceptance of a promise or affirmation" in lieu of the oath, besides other immunities, which were greatly appreciated by the Friends, though they were still liable to be drawn for military service.

Next to his more directly religious engagements the Bible Society shared by far the most largely his personal labours. For this cherished object he spared neither time nor strength. Holding the post of Depositary for about fifty years, nearly 250,000 Bibles passed through his hands.

The British Schools early claimed his attention, from a sense of the necessity of a better system of popular education which fastened upon him while teaching an adult school. The school-house at Cullercoats was his last effort of this kind, and may be looked upon as a monument of his energy and perseverance, when nearly eighty years of age.

The year before he was confined to his bed his thoughts were much occupied with the duty of the Society of Friends in the neglected cause of Foreign Missions; and he wrote with his own hand nearly a hundred letters to leading Friends in all parts of the country, urging them to a more active part in spreading the knowledge of the gospel in heathen lands. The subject engaged the earnest attention of the Yearly Meeting, so that when he was withdrawn from further active effort he was greatly cheered, saying— "The seed has taken root and *it will grow.*"

For two years he lay, often in pain but always cheerful, and brightly interested in passing events; but after a few days of rapidly declining strength, he passed to his reward. His interment was the last permitted in the grave-yard behind the Meeting House in Pilgrim Street, so closely associated with his life and work.

RACHEL PRIESTMAN.

JONATHAN PRIESTMAN.

Jonathan and Rachel Priestman.

1787-1863.   1791-1854.

JONATHAN PRIESTMAN was born at Malton, Yorkshire,
in 1787; his ancestors had been long settled at Thornton,
in the Vale of Pickering, and are known to have been
members of the Society of Friends as early as 1670.
Jonathan Priestman came to Newcastle-on-Tyne in 1808,
and in 1814 married Rachel Bragg, born in 1791, daughter
of Hadwen and Margaret Bragg. Her parents, anxious to
keep their daughter near them, enlarged and divided their
house at Summerhill so as to make a home for the young
people. Both houses were centres of many social and
religious interests. Jonathan and Rachel Priestman were
ministers of the Society of Friends, and much devoted
to service within its borders. Their door was ever open to
welcome anyone of whatever colour or creed whose errand
was of mercy to mankind, or for the advance of sound
opinions, however new or unpopular they might be.
Jonathan Priestman was one of the first teetotallers in
Newcastle, and took great interest in the establishment
of Infant Schools (then a new feature in educational
work), in Castle Garth, and the Orphan House, Brunswick
Square. Both he and his wife were indefatigable in the
Anti-Slavery movement, and were deeply interested in the
passing of the first Reform Bill, and in all measures for the
good of the country, as well as of their own town.

In 1843 Rachael Priestman went on a religious visit to
Friends in Philadelphia and parts of Pennsylvania, an
engagement which occupied about a year; the separation
was a close trial of faith to her and her husband.

Several times after her return they were united in
similar service in different parts of England.

In 1854 they set out together for the last time on a
visit to Friends in Ireland. At Waterford Rachel Priest-

man was taken ill, and died after a few weeks' illness in the house of Richard and Sarah Allen, surrounded by several members of her family, who received the utmost kindness and sympathy from the Friends among whom she had laboured. Jonathan Priestman lived nine years longer; his last illness was short. Always keenly alive to the interests around him, almost his last conscious question was to ask if the "Griswold," bringing a gift of corn from America to the famine-stricken workpeople in Lancashire, had reached our shores; and he spoke of carrying the news of Lincoln's Proclamation of Freedom, to the loved ones to whom he was hastening.

He died at Benwell on February 13th, 1863.

Edward Richardson—1805-1863.

The following memorial is an abridgement of Reminiscences written by his sister the late Ann R. Foster in 1876.

"OUR dear mother was left a widow in 1810, when my brother Edward was a boy of five years of age. Our home at Spring Gardens was a pleasant rural house, on the west side of the Castle Leazes, surrounded by ten acres of field and garden ground, around which very happy memories cling; at the week end it was the resort of our cousins and schoolfellows.

"My brother was always delicate, which made him an object of care and tender solicitude to his mother, to whom he was ever a dutiful and affectionate son.

"At the usual age he was sent as a day-scholar to John Bruce's school, where he was a favourite with his master, who considered him clever. For his age he excelled in Greek, which at that time was not much studied in day schools. After a few years he was sent to Frederick Smith's school at Darlington, which ranked as a first-class school in our Society, where he was placed

among the older pupils in the "class-room" with young
men who had almost a collegiate training, under an able
professor from the University of St. Andrews : he made
satisfactory progress in his studies, and took a good position
as a classical scholar.   On his return home he used to enjoy
reading Greek with Robert Foster, my husband's grandfather.

  " He worked as an apprentice in the tan-yard in
Newgate Street, in which he was afterwards to become
a partner, and gave his mind earnestly to his new
occupation.

  " As a young man he was fond of intellectual and
scientific pursuits, and enjoyed entertaining his young
friends with experiments in electricity and pneumatics.
Many a happy evening was spent in this way.   He
took a kind interest in the apprentices of the tan-
yard, ten or twelve in number, whom he used to invite to
his home when he read to them, and shewed them experiments with the electrifying machine and air pump.   His
manner towards the workmen was refined and courteous,
and he was much beloved by them.

  " We may now pass on to the time when he sought
the friendship of John Wigham's only daughter.   The
fame of her talents and accomplishments made an attempt
to obtain her hand, a somewhat anxious task.   His
visits to Edinburgh were times of great interest in
our family circle.   It was before the time of railways.
Our house stood by the North road, and the " Chevy Chase "
coach passed our gate, and when it stopped to take him up,
our little household would turn out to bid this beloved
brother good speed on his important errand.

  " In 1830, when he left the maternal roof, the blank
was keenly felt ; but his union with one possessing so
many estimable qualities. both of head and heart, was a
lasting blessing to himself and to our family.   She became
almost equally admired and beloved, and in her we

JANE RICHARDSON.

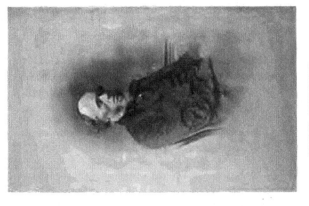

EDWARD RICHARDSON.

recognised to an extent rarely equalled the character of a Christian lady.

"On his marriage he took up his residence at Summer-hill Grove, then a country suburb of Newcastle with an uninterrupted view of Ravensworth and the valley of the Tyne.

"Throughout his life the tendency to pulmonary disease was a great drawback to his enjoyments and usefulness.

"When his large family were growing up around him, he was very watchful over them; he enjoyed mingling with his children in their pursuits, and taught them to be brave and daring, encouraging a spirit of self-reliance. He was fond of horseback exercise himself, and trained them when young in the love of it; his manner towards them was gentle and kindly. It was his desire to train them in the principles of the Society of Friends, to which he was himself sincerely attached. In a letter written to them in 1857, found after his decease, he says, ' In all your actions seek to approve yourself unto God, your Heavenly Father. Cultivate all the Christian graces. If you should, in a day of disputation, be called upon to examine the foundation of your outward Christian profession, do it in meekness and fear, and recollect the principle of the profession in which you have been brought up, a principle that will lead you *not* into austerities and formalities, but into a renunciation of the vanities and fashions of the world. May you all ever live in the fear of God, loving our Lord Jesus in sincerity, and may you be sanctified by the operations of the Holy Spirit.'

"His weak health prevented his close attention to business; but his brother John, who was his partner, kindly and willingly liberated him, whenever it was thought desirable for him to leave home. He spent the winter of 1836-7 with his family at Torquay, and there his son John Wigham was born. He took many journeys for the benefit of his health, both by sea and land, when it was frequently my pleasure to be his companion. On one of these occasions we were shipwrecked. In 1837 we went to London by the Menai steamer to consult Sir James Clark, who recommended him to return home by a sailing vessel. Accordingly we embarked in a Newcastle trader, " The Bywell," making her first voyage.

" The weather was threatening, and the captain crowded on all sail; hoping to have light enough to run into Yarmouth Roads and shelter for the night. But the storm of wind and rain increased. My dear brother and I were alone about six o'clock in the cabin, fearing no danger, when suddenly there came an awful shock, quickly followed by another and another. The vessel had struck upon the Newcombe Sands, and all hope that the ship would get off was taken away, for the rudder was soon lost, and she seemed to be breaking up by the violence of the waves. The men prepared to launch the boats; the first was swamped in the attempt, and the long boat shared the same fate. We were three miles from shore.

" We were about three hours in this state of exposure and uncertainty, when the lifeboat from Lowestoft, with seventeen brave men, came to our rescue. We reached the shore at about ten o'ciock at night, where we received most kind attention from the Vicar of Lowestoft, Francis Cunningham, and his excellent lady, one of the Gurneys of Earlham. He took us to their house, and kindly sent us on to Norwich in their carriage to take coach for the North.

" Here then let me commemorate the loving kindness of the Lord, how He graciously upheld us, and preserved us in this great danger.

" My brother's family having become too large for the house in Summerhill Grove, he removed his residence in 1852 to Beech Grove, which was more in the country, and was surrounded by a pleasant garden and field. The house was large enough to allow of its being divided, so that I could occupy a part of it, and we lived very happily as close neighbours for six years.

"My dear brother was concerned for his own spiritual condition, and has left on record some deep self-examinations. On 1st mo. 12th, 1854 he writes:—' This being my birthday I have been looking over a few scattered memoranda made in some of my former birthdays, and I am afresh reminded of the great goodness of God to me in the lengthening out of my days, in the prolonged gift of an affectionate wife, in the health and well-doing of my children, in the abundance of earthly goods, in kind friends, in placing me in a land of freedom, where the word of God may have free course. What lacketh? the quickening beams of Thy love, O Lord, upon my soul.'

"In 1856: Grant O Lord! that when the awful messenger is sent to me, I may be found ready, with my loins girded, and having on the wedding garment. Let me be found calm and free from harrassing worldly cares.

"12th mo. 2nd, 1857: This day last week the District Bank resolved to suspend payment." It is a dire calamity; my brother and I are both shareholders! After further comments he adds, "As to myself I have also been favoured with some ability to draw near to the Throne of Grace, and to feel the overshadowings of Divine Mercy, so that I have been ready to conclude that my loss may turn out to the profit of my soul, and I humbly trust that for the remaining period of my life, I may be blessed with the influences of the Lord's Holy Spirit, and that finally I may be permitted to receive the white robe, and to enter the kingdom of peace and joy. Amen.

"6 mo., 20th, 1858: First day evening: we are all assembled at home, and enjoying this pretty place, Beech Grove, which we expect soon to leave for a smaller house. What depths have I been in during the last half year! but how much have they drawn me towards the Great Source of happiness, of power, and of love!

"Some years ago I was startled in looking at the plates in Scott's "Bunyan's Pilgrim's Progress" to observe the man falling into the Silver Mine. If I have unwittingly been setting up Idols of Silver or Gold, they are now thrown down: may I seek to draw nearer and nearer to God!

"In 1860, he and his family removed to South Ashfield, where he resided until his death.

"In the early morning of the 13th February, 1863, the tanyard in Newgate Street was destroyed by fire. He bore this fresh catastrophe with great resignation and calmness. He had intended to go on the 24th with his family to Gilsland for a little change, but during the night he was seized with severe pain, and on the following day was very weak, and not suffered to converse. On the 26th, as I sat by his bed-side I was distressed to see him look so very ill, but he spoke a few words to me cheerfully. On his son John going to take leave of him for the night he said to him very impressively yet cheerily, 'John, my lad! I wish thee to know that when my Maker calls me to him, I shall go joyfully, yes joyfully!' It was arranged that his eldest daughter, Anna Deborah, should watch by him during the night. He passed the hours quietly until about four o'clock in the morning, when he took a fit of coughing, and suddenly died in her arms, as she was supporting his head.

"We doubt not that the white robe, for which he so often, and so earnestly prayed, was granted to him; and, arrayed in that robe, the Righteousness of Christ his Saviour, that he was ready with his lamp trimmed, when the midnight cry came, 'Behold the Bridegroom cometh, go ye out to meet him.'

"His memory is fondly cherished."

The foregoing narrative makes frequent mention of Jane Richardson, but it is due to her beautiful character and to the important influence she exercised over a wide circle in such a variety of ways during her married life to add the following brief extracts from the account prepared for the "Annual Monitor," by her cousin Eliza Wigham:—

Jane Richardson, 1808=1873,

"JANE RICHARDSON was the only child of John Wigham, of Edinburgh, and a grand-daughter of John Wigham, of Coanwood, in Northumberland."

John Wigham (junior, as her father was usually styled), was three years old when his parents migrated to Scotland. He was highly esteemed as a man of expanded views, and of large hospitalities. His daughter was thus early introduced to influences which developed her highly sympathetic character; and though lonely as a child, she had no taint of selfishness. Her taste for intellectual pursuits, her poetic gift, and her early friendships made her girlhood very happy.

In 1830 she was married to Edward Richardson. She most conscientiously performed the duties devolving upon her as wife and mother, and as mistress in the household. The education of her children claimed her earnest care.

The uncertain and delicate health of her husband was a source of great solicitude, producing a tendency to early blindness which in after years was realised. Her many trials and sorrows begat in her a wonderful power of sympathy. Even strangers were so drawn to her that, almost before they were aware, they told her their troubles. James Montgomery, the poet, had in 1837 established in Newcastle, a [Society for visiting aged women. She took one of the poorest districts in the town, and continued diligent in the work till her increasing blindness rendered it impossible.

In 1853, during the terrible visitation of Asiatic cholera, Jane Richardson was fearless in visiting the worst houses and cheering those who were stricken with panic.

M

She acknowledged it as a great favour at such a time to be preserved in quiet trust in the Preserver of men, free from nervous alarm.

Consequent upon the failure of the Bank involving the family in pecuniary losses, her patience, faith, and courage were exercised in needful retrenchments which helped her husband through the dreary months.

In the autumn of 1863 came a heavy trial in the death of her husband, but his bereaved partner was able even to rejoice in her sorrow. She was, in her general life, of a hopeful and gladsome spirit. It seemed as if it were given her to illustrate the principle of gladness, which she thought was sometimes wanting in the daily routine and in the public worship of even devoted Friends; even in her blindness, her powers of memory and imagination were such, that a stranger walking with her in the cherished scenery of Grasmere or Scotland, would hardly realise that she could no longer see the objects of which she spoke so enthusiastically.

After a few years of declining health, borne with marked Christian fortitude, and after fluctuations of sickness, extreme weakness, and unconsciousness, she gently expired on the morning of the third of twelfth month.

Her face, which during that year of illness had gained much dignity and sweetness, bore the impress of perfect peace, as if she might have said, "I have seen God's hand through a life time, and all was for the best."

JONATHAN AND ANN DREWRY.

Jonathan Drewry—1795-1865.
Ann Drewry—1799-1877.

JONATHAN DREWRY was the son of Nixon and Elizabeth Drewry, of Cockermouth. He was apprenticed to his uncle, Daniel Oliver, tea dealer, in the Bigg Market, in 1811. After his marriage, he commenced business as tea dealer and grocer on the Sandhill, Newcastle, previous to his establishment as a sharebroker, in which business he continued to the time of his death, in 1865, at the Priory, in Summerhill Grove, where he had resided for more than twenty years.

ANN DREWRY, daughter of James and Esther Hudson, of the Cragg, near Setmurthy, Bassenthwaite.

SARAH ROBINSON.

Christopher Robinson— -1833.
Sarah Robinson—1779-1866.

SARAH ROBINSON was the daughter of Jonathan and Esther Harris, and was born at "Green," in the parish of Lamplugh, county of Cumberland, in 1779. Her father's family had been members of the Society of Friends from an early period, and there still exists the marriage certificate of Sarah Harris's great grandfather, Thomas Harris, who was married at Pardshaw Meeting in 1690. This Thomas Harris may have heard George Fox preach at Pardshaw Craig. Sarah Harris's father, Jonathan Harris, was what in Cumberland was usually called a "statesman," that is, he farmed land belonging to himself. The family attended

Pardshaw Meeting, usually walking the distance of two or three miles. The farmhouse of "Green" still exists, and is sometimes visited by descendants of the family; but the locality and its surroundings are much changed since the discovery of large deposits of iron ore.

Early in the present century Sarah Harris went to Eaglesfield, near Cockermouth, to live with Elihu and Ruth Robinson during their declining years. The memory of Elihu Robinson, long cherished by old Cumberland Friends, has been revived in late years by the publication of the life of John Dalton, to whom he was of great service in early life. In this home Sarah Harris met with persons of superior endowments. Friends, as well as others, and she would often recall the visits of Thomas Clarkson, the Abolitionist, and of Thomas Wilkinson, a Quaker Poet, and a friend of Wordsworth. The home of Elihu Robinson was broken up on the death of the survivor, but the house is still pointed out by the villagers.

In 1812, Sarah Harris was married to Christopher Robinson, and Newcastle was henceforth her home. For a few years they lived over the shop (now demolished) at the head of the Side, but afterwards moved to a house in South Street, without the town walls and in the near neighbourhood of the Forth. This situation was then pleasant enough but, in the course of a few years, much of the adjacent land was leased for foundries, gas works, and the works of R. Stephenson and Co. The dwelling house is now included in the latter, and used for offices.

Christopher Robinson died in 1833, and his widow continued to reside in Newcastle until her death in 1866, aged 86 years. This long widowhood was not unattended by trouble and sorrow, but she held fast her confidence firm unto the end. She was much attached to the Society of Friends both from early association and mature conviction, and may be regarded as a typical representative of the Friend of a bygone age.

William Beaumont,—1790-1869,

WAS born in 1790, and died at Newcastle in 1869.

He was the son of John Beaumont of Battersea Rise, Surrey. The neighbourhood of Battersea has been much changed since those days, but the old house at Battersea Rise is still standing, and was, until lately, the property of a granddaughter of John Beaumont. The next house was, at the beginning of the century, the home of William Wilberforce.

The Beaumonts are a Yorkshire family, coming originally from the West Riding, near Pontefract, but as William Beaumont never married, and the only daughters of his two brothers both died unmarried, this branch of the family has left no descendants of the name.

William Beaumont came to the North as a young man, and settled in Newcastle, going into the leather business there, as so many Newcastle Friends had done before him.

His two brothers remained in the South; the eldest, Abraham, living at Stamford Hill, and the youngest, John, at Ufford, in Suffolk. The two sisters came to the North, Elizabeth marrying Joseph Pease of Feethams, Darlington; and Sarah coming to Newcastle, lived with her brother William until her death in 1840.

To those members of Newcastle Meeting who can look back for 35 or 40 years, it will not be difficult, with the aid of the portrait here given, to recall the upright figure, the clear, healthy complexion, and white hair of the elderly Friend, who was accustomed, with great regularity, to occupy the corner seat on the left, just under the Ministers' gallery of the Newcastle Friends' Meeting House.

William Beaumont required to be well known to be appreciated and understood. There was a certain amount

WILLIAM BEAUMONT.

of coldness in his manner, and a little formality and dignity in his address, which made it difficult to approach him at first, but to those who broke through this outward reserve a warm heart and a most affectionate nature were discovered and there was a loyalty in the friendships he formed which made them very close and lasting, and greatly valued.

It was a delight to him, in his early Newcastle days, to leave his business for a time, and with an intimate friend and companion set off for a few weeks' holiday in Scotland, or in the South, when he would revel in the beauty of nature; and later in life, he yearly planned excursions with his nephew and niece at Darlington, and as time went on extended his holiday invitations to a younger generation still. Dr. Brady of Gateshead, John Crossfield of Windermere, and several others were his frequent companions for years, and many were the journeys they undertook together.

A singularly just and upright man in his dealings with all, he was greatly esteemed by his fellow-townsmen. He became much attached to the town of his adoption, and was a very regular and useful member of the Infirmary Committee, and of some of the other charities of the North.

A man who disliked a crowd, but loved his individual friends. A man of most methodical habits and orderly ways, with a quiet sense of humour and a great enjoyment of books. A keen observer, and a good judge of character. A lover of his own little church, but with a heart large enough to see and feel the good in the religion of his neighbours.

A most considerate man to his servants and all his fellows. Very anxious to avoid giving trouble during the whole of his life, he extended the same care even to his executors, an unusual mark of consideration.

"My books and my papers are all in order. You will not have any difficulty in winding up my affairs. I have destroyed what it was not needful to keep. You will find only two letters in my writing table."

These were almost the last words to his acting executor. And when the two letters were discovered after his death, one of them was from the elder brother Abraham, a young man just beginning his career in the South, addressed to his younger brother William, a boy of 17, giving in few words much good advice, and exhorting him to begin and to end his life by doing justly, by loving mercy, and by walking all his days very humbly with his God. Advice which had been carefully treasured up in the keeping of this faded letter during a long life, and which those who could judge were well aware had not been given in vain.

Joseph Watson—1807-1874.

JOSHUA WATSON'S eldest son Joseph (alluded to above), was born on the 4th day of ninth month 1807. Margaret Bragg is one of the signatories to the certificate as having been present at his birth. He was educated at Ackworth School for rather more than a year; but in those days the discipline was severe and unsuited to those boys who had special attractions at home, and he was not sorry to leave it. When his younger brothers met him at the coach office they refused to walk home with "the funny little old man" (as the gamins of that day called him), scarcely nine years old, but attired in broad-brimmed beaver hat, Friend's coat and vest with brass buttons, knee breeches, grey stockings, and shoes with plain buckles. He went afterwards to the famous school at Darlington kept by the Brothers Cowan. Here he was in a more congenial atmosphere, and made great progress under those enlightened masters. His remarkable memory retained throughout life much of the Greek and Latin poets, with whose words he then became familiar.

At those two schools he made many life-long friendships; among these, those which he most prized were with William Howitt and John Bright.

JOSEPH WATSON.

After leaving school he became clerk in Backhouse and Company's Bank, where he remained for nearly two years, gaining that knowledge of accounts which enabled him afterwards to take a leading part in all legal enquiries in which figures were involved. He had an unusual gift for mental arithmetic and he never lost this. In 1860 he had a contest with Mr. Bidder, the famous calculating boy, in which he came off victorious. Wishing to have a more independent life he was articled to Messrs. Kirkley and Fenwick, a well-known firm of solicitors, and spent the year 1829-30 in London, attending law lectures by Professor Amos at University College, then recently opened.

He took the first prize in the term examination, and the second prize in the final examination, beating, amongst others, Mr. Whiteside, afterwards the famous Irish judge.

In 1835 he married Sarah, daughter of Robert and Mary Spence, of North Shields, and had the blessing with her of a happy thirty-six years' union.

He had considerable literary powers, and wrote one thing at least, "The Ballad of the Worme of Lambton," which is still popular and is constantly reprinted. He was a tolerably regular contributor for some years to "Tait's Edinburgh Magazine," and the anti-slavery album called the "Bow in the Cloud," and that produced by the young Friends of this district some seventy years ago, entitled "The Aurora Borealis," have important poems by him; and the latter one of the few quaker stories which have been written by a Friend and full of the right quaker atmosphere. He had a rare talent for epigram, and did good work with it upon many occasions.

His great love of children led him to write many a pretty story for their delectation. He was quite happy when he could have a children's party, eight or ten wee ones, all to himself, shewing them toys and telling them tales.

He was an ardent lover of civil and religious liberty; and his rare oratorical gift made him a powerful ally of the

Liberal party in the mighty struggles which went forward in the late Twenties and early Thirties. His speeches in favour of Catholic Emancipation, the Abolition of Slavery in the West Indies, and the Reform Bill, are filled not merely with eloquent passages (which indeed abound) but with the glow of generous conviction. As he advanced in years his public appearances became rare, but his Liberal convictions strengthened. Never was he heard to greater advantage than when in 1868 he took the leading part at a public breakfast, given in the Assembly Rooms, Newcastle, to William Lloyd Garrison. It was indeed a meeting of brave old men, eloquent once again in the cause for which they had fought so stoutly for so many years, side by side, though in distant lands.

He took a leading part in the return of John Bright for Durham, was secretary to the great Anti-Corn Law Bazaar, and local secretary to the Exhibition of 1851, and for many years was chairman of the Fine Arts Society, and secretary of the Literary and Philosophical Society of Newcastle.

Though one who spoke little about religious matters, his voice was always raised on the side of righteousness, and his quiet but effectual testimony to the truth carried conviction into many quarters where such teaching is but seldom received.

He died on the 14th of twelfth month, 1874, his wife and two of his sons having preceded him by but brief spaces of time. Shortly before his death he wrote several poems of much beauty, breathing that spirit of Christian resignation which he had in life so truly exemplified.

Charles Bragg,—1801-1874,

THE youngest of Hadwen and Margaret Bragg's children, was born at Newcastle, in 1801. Having been educated at Friends' Schools in Leeds and Tottenham, he was apprenticed to his father's business in Pilgrim Street.

SUSANNAH H. BRAGG.

CHARLES BRAGG.

A great admirer of the beautiful in Nature and in Art, the details of business were not to his taste; but with a conscientious obedience to duty he was diligent in attending to it.

His father died when he was nineteen, and in later days he used to allude to this loss and to the care which it brought upon him.

Riding tours in the Border counties, visiting the romantic scenes of Scott's tales, or the homes of Burns and of Hogg, were enjoyed recreations. The sea-side also was a favourite resort, and the welfare of the fishermen, amongst whom he had some esteemed friends, was always interesting to him.

The institutions in Newcastle, which his father had assisted in establishing, had his continued interest and help.

In 1835 he married Susannah H. Balkwill, of Plymouth, who had frequently paid long visits to her sister, Sarah Richardson, of Summerhill Grove. After his mother's death, he lived at Summerhill until he removed to Lintz Green, a pleasant country home in the valley of the Derwent the quiet seclusion of which was much appreciated after the business cares of the day. His daily drives to or from town were well suited to his enjoyment of natural beauty.

The early death of their beloved and only son, just as he was of age to relieve his father, was a bitter sorrow which weighed heavily upon his heart, but the tendency to depression resulting from this grief was overcome by Divine grace, and his latest days are remembered as among the brightest by those who were privileged to know him intimately.

He held the position of an elder for several years.

His death took place at Lintz Green in 1874.

Thomas Potts—1786–1876.

THOMAS POTTS was a remarkable man in many ways.

He was an old man-of-war's-man, became a Friend, and was employed as foreman or manager of Jonathan Priestman's glue works.

It is related of him that once when someone said something disparaging of his employer, he threw himself into a sparring attitude, and casting off his coat, exclaimed : " There goes Tommy, the Quaker ! Now, come on."

A memorandum made by Anna Deborah Richardson, between whom and Thomas Potts there existed a singular friendship, relates a conversation, thus :—

This afternoon Thomas Potts called and said he wished to pay me a little visit, as he thought it might be the last time he would be able to do so.

He spoke a good deal of the necessity of Christian self-denial ; of the poor man giving up ardent spirits and tobacco, and subscribing a shilling or more a week, first to the Bible Society, that the minds of the people may be enlightened ; next, to colporteurs to distribute the word of God ; then to district missionaries ; then to Schools : and if the rich would do likewise in proportion to their means ! then we might hope, firmly, to see the world evangelized : but Friends are too supine, too un-energetic.

" I said I thought the minds of Christians would be crushed down too heavily by the knowledge of the thousands of outcasts apparently beyond what are called the means of grace, if it were not for the revelation of a Divine Teacher to be listened to in the heart. He agreed, and said this testimony of the early Quakers was not yet fully preached ; that it ought to go hand-in-hand with the doctrine of the Atonement, for without this grace of inward teaching, how could man be accountable ? "

Then followed a story of simple trust and of clear answers to prayer experienced by a very poor man living

THOMAS POTTS.

in Gallowgate. I made some remark on the fulness of
the prayer 'Give us this day our daily bread.' Thomas
Potts said that he believed such reward as the above was
only granted to the true and faithful Israelite ; and that
where such trust was wanting, there would be a turning
and an overturning ; a turning again and an overturning,
until it was attained ; and that the Christian needed to be
baptised with the baptism his Lord was baptized with, and
drink of the same cup of utter hatred to sin, if he hoped to
sit with Him in His Kingdom. " If," he said, " I hear
words of evil, even the name of the Great Intelligence,
spoken lightly, I cannot bear it. I go up to the offender
and lay my hand upon his shoulder and say : ' My dear
friend, oh do not speak so in the company of Thomas
Potts' ; and I feel as though a wool-carder were drawn
down my nerves, and a dagger plunged into my heart."

" A great deal more he said in the same way, full of.
feeling and of the most earnest desires for the good of the
race. In going away, he said, with the tears rolling down
his cheeks, ' I may never see thee again ; but if a few
hours of lightsomeness from the weight on my head should
ever be granted me, I will write to thee, indeed I will."

Daniel Oliver—1806-1878.

WAS the son of Daniel and Mary Oliver (see page 130). He
carried on the grocery business established by his father,
the friendship between whom and George Richardson was
warmly continued by their sons, whose shops were only a
few doors further down the street. D. Oliver was one of
the earliest to embrace total abstinence, and was a staunch
supporter of this cause all his life.

He married Ann Noble, of Scotby, near Carlisle. In
1870 they removed with their daughters to Jersey, where
they resided in retirement for about eight years and after a

N

DANIEL   OLIVER.

happy union, in death they were not divided. They fell
asleep in Jesus on the same day in 1878, the 24th of third
month, the 49th anniversary of their wedding day.

Henry Clapham—1827-1883.

HENRY CLAPHAM was a son of the late Anthony
Clapham, and was born at Benwell Grove, Newcastle-on-
Tyne, 25th February, 1827. His father's family were well
known on Tyneside as chemical manufacturers, Clapham's
chimney at the Friars Goose Chemical Works being sixty
years ago one of the wonders of the district; it was at
that time the highest chimney in England. He was
educated at a small school at Durham, and used to
frequently relate how quiet was the condition of Durham
meeting at that time, the silence being seldom broken. He
married in 1859 Esther Mary Watson, second daughter of
the late Joseph Watson, of Bensham Grove. Like his
father, he devoted himself to commercial pursuits, carrying
on a large merchant's and shipowner's business, was chairman of Newcastle Exchange, treasurer and vice-president
of the Chamber of Commerce. He always took a warm
interest in the work of the Society of Friends, and was for
many years Superintendent of the Sabbath School at the
Manors. He was also an Overseer of Newcastle Meeting,
and took a special interest in the work of the Home
Mission, and was one of the chief promoters of the Eldon
Mission.

He was identified with several philanthropic and social
movements, amongst which might be mentioned the Ragged
and Industrial Schools, the Shipwrecked Mariners' Widows
and Orphans' Society, Model Dwellings for the Poor, Soup
Kitchen, Young Men's and Young Women's Christian Asso-
ciations. He was the main instrument, through the
generosity of Mr. R. S. Donkin, in getting All Saints'

HENRY CLAPHAM.

churchyard laid out as a public garden, which was a great boon to the poor of that neighbourhood. His last act in connection with philanthropic work was the formation of a Home for Young Women engaged in business. He was closely associated with the public life of the district, being one of the representatives of Elswick Ward for many years in the City Council. He was also a representative of the Dues Payers on the River Tyne Commission, a Justice of the Peace, and was appointed Sheriff of Newcastle in November, 1882, being probably the first Quaker in this city to hold the office. He died during his Shrievalty on the 4th of June, 1883, aged 56.

henry Brady—1805-1883.
hannah Brady—1802-1872.

HENRY BRADY, son of Thomas and Elizabeth Brady, of Staindrop, was born there on the 13th of ninth month, 1805. He was educated at Ackworth and Darlington, and after receiving a training as a Medical Student in London, he settled in Gateshead in the year 1829.

He was possessed of much intellectual power, and, though naturally quick, impulsive and critical, he soon took a useful position in our Society. As years advanced he appeared gradually but surely to yield to the softening and refining influence of the Holy Spirit.

In 1831, he married Hannah, daughter of Ebenezer and Ann Bowman, of One Ash Grange, Derbyshire, whose gentle, retiring disposition and ready sympathy endeared her to a large circle of friends and acquaintances. She was indefatigable in her efforts for the welfare of her large family, entering into their pursuits with the keenest interest; and in times of trial and adversity, by her cheerfulness and unrepining fortitude, was a tower of strength both to her husband and children, encouraging them to look beyond the fleeting things of this life and proving, by her daily example, that her treasure was in heaven and that her hopes were centred there.

They both filled the office of Elder acceptably for many years; and in 1861, when past middle life Henry Brady yielded to a call to the ministry which was recognized by his friends as from the Lord. This was at a time when the meetings were generally held in silence, which made the effort greater. His communications were neither long nor frequent, but gave evidence of the true baptism of the Holy Spirit, and his prayers were offered with marked reverence and fervency.

HANNAH BRADY.

HENRY BRADY.

He was earnestly solicitous that our Meetings should be times of deep spiritual worship, and rarely allowed his close professional engagements to prevent his attendance, at least once every First-day; at the small gatherings also, during the week, his ministry was often felt to be especially instructive. He was emphatically a Christian physician, often saying a helpful word or offering a prayer on behalf of his patients when caring for their bodily infirmities.

His wife was an active worker in many of the charitable agencies of Gateshead, some of which were continued to the end of her life; and her unselfishness and practical help were most valuable in many cases of need which she heard of in the course of her husband's practice.

In 1859, the loss of considerable property, the savings of many laborious years, just when he was on the point of retiring from the active duties of his profession, was borne by Henry Brady and his wife with unrepining patience; and when she was taken from him by death in 1872, his christian resignation was signally manifested. She was tenderly beloved, and the trial was severe, but he remarked to one of his daughters, " Do not think that I am impatient to go to mother, I hope I am quite willing either to go or stay as God sees right."

He was always careful not to speak against the character of any one, and to check such remarks when he heard them, saying " Is there nothing *good* to say of him."

His conversation with his family shewed that he had no trust in any righteousness of his own, but that it was through unmerited mercy that he was accepted through the blood of his Saviour.

On the 14th of seventh month, 1883, he peacefully entered into his everlasting rest.

ELIZABETH PROCTER.

JOSEPH PROCTER.

Joseph Procter—1800-1875.
Elizabeth Procter—1809-1886.

JOSEPH PROCTER was the son of Joseph and Elizabeth
Proctor, of North Shields, his mother being one of the large
family of John Richardson, of the Low Lights Tannery.

He was a flour miller, first at the celebrated mill at
Willington, and afterwards at Newcastle, and had the
reputation for such strict uprightness in his trade transactions as won the respect of customers, competitors, and
all with whom he came in contact.

He married in 1831 Elizabeth Carr of Kendal, sister of
Jonathan Dodgson Carr, the founder of the biscuit factory
at Carlisle.

After leaving Willington they resided at North Shields,
and finally at Gosforth, becoming members of Newcastle
Meeting in 1865.

Joseph Procter was a highly valued supporter of the
discipline of the Society, and both he and his wife filled
various responsible offices in these relations.

Their gentleness and kind Christian courtesy won for
them warm places in the hearts of their friends.

The following appeared in Mrs. Boyce's " Records of
a Quaker Family," and there are many who can bear witness
to the truthfulness of the description.

" Joseph Procter was a man who delighted in theo-
logical studies and in abstruse speculations, and who, in
spite of his constitutional diffidence, did not fear to differ
from his fellows on many points. In the intense spirituality
of his devotion, in his amiable disposition, and in his blame-
less life, he was a true Friend. His mind was one in
which the imaginative and contemplative faculties pre-
dominated."

Henry Bowman Brady—1835-1891.

Extracted from "Nature."

WAS born on February 23, 1835, at Gateshead. His father, an esteemed medical practitioner of that place, belonged to the Society of Friends, and retained to the end the dress and manner of conversation of that body.

After an ordinary school career spent in Yorkshire and Lancashire, and an apprenticeship under the late Mr. T. Harvey, of Leeds. and some further study at Newcastle in the laboratory of Dr. T. Richardson, which may be considered as the forerunner of the present Newcastle College of Science, he started business in that city as a pharmaceutical chemist in 1855, while yet a minor. He conducted it with such ability that in 1876 he felt able to resign it to Mr. N. H Martin, and to devote the whole of his time to scientific work.

He contributed to science in two ways—one direct, the other indirect. Of the many scientific movements of the last thirty years or so, one of not the least remarkable has been the scientific development of the pharmaceutical chemist. Into that movement Brady threw himself with great vigour, especially in his earlier years. He was for many years on the Council of the Pharmaceutical Society, and the progress of that body was greatly helped by his wide knowledge of science and of scientific men and things, as well as by his calm and unprejudiced judgment.

His more direct contributions to science were in the form of researches in natural history, more especially on the Foraminifera. His first publication seems to have been a contribution in 1863 to the British Association as a report on the dredging of the Northumberland coast and Dogger Bank ; his last was a paper which appeared only a short time ago. Between these two he published a large number of researches, including a monograph on Carboniferous and

HENRY BOWMAN BRADY.

Permian Foraminifera, an exhaustive report on the Foraminifera of the *Challenger* Expedition, as well as monographs
on Parkeria and Loftusia, and on Polymorphina, in which
he was joint author.

By these works he not only established a position, both
in this country and abroad, as one of the highest authorities

on the subject, but, what is of more importance, largely
advanced our knowledge. Every one of his papers is
characterized by the most conscientious accuracy and
justice; and though his attention was largely directed to
classification and to the morphological points therein
involved, his mind, as several of his papers indicate, was
also occupied with the wider problems of morphological and
biological interest which the study of these lowly forms
suggests.

The leisure of the last fifteen years gave him opportunity for travel, and he visited various parts of the world,
utilizing many of his journeys—notably one to the Pacific
Ocean—in the collection and study of Foraminifera. Some
of these travels were undertaken on the score of health, to
avoid the evils of an English winter, for he was during
many years subject to chronic pulmonary mischief.

During his last journey for this purpose—one to the
Nile in the winter of 1889-90—he met with difficulties, and
failed to receive the benefit from the change which he had
secured on former occasions. During the last two or three
years, and especially during the last year, his condition gave
increasing anxiety to his friends; the malady against which
he had so long struggled seemed to be beating him at last;
and we heard with sorrow rather than with surprise that
the fierceness of the recent cold had conquered him. Settled
for the winter at Bournemouth, and full of cheerful hopes
for the coming summer, he succumbed to a sudden attack of
inflammation of the lungs, and died on January 10, 1891.

Science has lost a steady and fruitful worker, and
many men of science have lost a friend and a helpmate
whose place they feel no one else can fill. His wide
knowledge of many branches of scientific inquiry, and his
large acquaintance with scientific men, made the hours
spent with him always profitable; his sympathy with art
and literature, and that special knowledge of men and
things which belongs only to the travelled man, made him

welcome also where science was unknown; while the brave patience with which he bore the many troubles of enfeebled health, his unselfish thoughtfulness for interests other than his own, and a sense of humour which, when needed, led him to desert his usual staid demeanour for the merriment of the moment, endeared him to all his friends.

Henry Richardson—1806-1885.
Anna H. Richardson—1806-1892.

ANNA RICHARDSON was the daughter of Samuel and Esther Atkins, of Chipping Norton. Her mother was a saintly woman—one who resorted much to earnest prayer for herself and her family.

The sweetness and beauty of the Oxfordshire home were a treasured memory, and there the seeds were sown of that philanthropy which so remarkably characterised her in after days. She writes,—

"I believe it was at sixteen years of age my mind was awakened to the importance of a clearer recognition of Gospel-truth and of unseen things; and by twenty-one the study of the Holy Scriptures had become a subject of loving and very deep interest."

In the summer of 1833 Anna Atkins was united in marriage with Henry Richardson, of Newcastle.

In early life he passed through a period of spiritual doubt, and his attachment to the Society of Friends was somewhat disturbed. Divine grace and the wise counsels of his father were helpful in this time of difficulty, and he was completely re-established on the true foundation.

When brought into the wider sphere of her new home, Anna Richardson felt the restraints at that time customary in the Society of Friends to be rather out of harmony with her own conceptions of Christian liberty, and she occasionally reverted in later years to the check which was then put

ANNA H. RICHARDSON.

HENRY RICHARDSON.

upon some of those ministries in which she was prepared to engage. But, notwithstanding these early difficulties, they became closely attached and earnest members of the Society; and, though in later life prevented by physical disabilities from the attendance of meetings for Discipline and larger gatherings, they accepted the offices of Overseer and Elder, and maintained a bright and helpful intercourse with their fellow members, manifesting a warm interest in those who joined the Society from the working classes.

Anna Richardson says:—" In 1834, I think it was, that, at the suggestion of dear Elizabeth Fry, I became a regular visitor at the Newcastle prison. It was a mournful duty, but was maintained more or less for many years. I remember it as the time when I first became a 'teetotaller,' for which there was evidently a call in such a position.

" I may thankfully record that we were enabled to give a helping hand in commencing the Friends' Sabbath School at Newcastle, and my dear husband was for several years its superintendent."

H. and A. Richardson were always warm adherents of the Anti-Slavery Society. The arrival of Frederick Douglas in England in 1845, and his eloquent appeals on behalf of his suffering people led to an increased effort for their liberation.

For several years they edited two periodicals in the interests of peace:—the " Olive Leaf " specially for children, and the " Peace Advocate," for general circulation. In connection with this cause, so dear to their hearts, A.H.R. writes :—" The summer of 1849 was a memorable one, for we joined a large party from England in attending the Peace Congress at Paris.

" Previous to this our minds had been much drawn to the importance of the Holy Scriptures being more largely circulated amongst the people. After returning home the subject rested much with us, and we consulted the French Consul, as to the possibility of gaining access to France with that object in view. He said he felt sure it could be done, but 'Go yourselves,' he added, 'and make the distribution a personal one.'" Continuing the narrative, she says:—" It seemed best to follow his advice. The needful money was readily given by kind friends, and 2,000 copies of the New Testament were specially bound, with a suitable inscription in each for presentation."

The following spring H. and A. Richardson set out, accompanied by their cousin, Ann Richardson (now Foster) and Eliza Nichol, and they had the great satisfaction of distributing the books themselves. The Testaments were gratefully received by all parties, many of them in high stations.

Henry Richardson was much concerned for the welfare of the ragged children frequenting the streets of Newcastle, and promoted the establishment of a Boys' Ragged School. This has since been developed into the Industrial Schools for both boys and girls.

He may be said to have inherited a personal interest in the work of Bible distribution, having the depôt on his shop premises, and voluntarily sharing the labours of depositary. Soon after his retirement from business in 1858, the depôt was removed to Pilgrim Street, and there he continued to attend regularly until within a short time of his death, which occurred at his residence in Park Road, in 1885.

The six years of widowhood which were allotted to A. Richardson were spent almost entirely in the sweet rest and contentment of her much loved home. She sat busily occupied with her pen, and a large correspondence was maintained with distant members of her family, many of them on the other side of the Atlantic, and with friends and others on philanthropic matters.

A sudden failure in the heart's action on the 12th of Third month, 1892, caused her relatives alarm; it was evident that the aged frame had received a check from which it could not recover. She quickly realised that the call had come, and gently passed away.

Frederick Clark—1822-1892.
Phebe Clark—1828-1883.

FREDERICK CLARK was born at Oakham on the 30th of Third month, 1822. He was educated at York School, and when about sixteen years of age was apprenticed to a Friend, as a draper, at Newcastle. When his apprenticeship expired he lived a year or two at Leeds, and then commenced business at Gateshead. He subsequently entered into business as a chemical manufacturer, being well known and greatly respected in commercial life.

In 1851 he married Phebe Goundry, a union of great happiness till broken by her death in 1883. He filled a useful post as honorary secretary to the Gateshead Auxiliary Bible Society for many years, evincing a warm personal interest in its work.

A number of years after taking up his residence in Newcastle he took an active part in the Friends' Adult School which, with his persevering assistance, made a decided advance. After years of patient labour a Mission Meeting on First-day evenings was commenced in connection with the school. He entered warmly into this effort, and never allowed his personal comfort to interfere with his regular attendance. His interest in these efforts ended only with his life. He and his colleagues also commenced a Mission in Victoria Street, where Cottage Meetings were held. One of his co-workers writes:—" God blessed his labours very abundantly, as many can testify to the blessing they received by his ministry." There was one very pleasing feature of his character, the good gift of making all feel at home in his company, and thus cementing a Christian relationship so essential to the strengthening of the Christian life. Nothing seemed to damp his ardour when he was about his Father's business.

FREDERICK CLARK.

PHEBE CLARK.

He was helpful in the discipline of the Society, serving as Overseer most efficiently for several years, and afterwards as a faithful Elder; never allowing his retiring nature to prevent his undertaking duties from which he would rather have been excused.

Frederick and Phebe Clark took a very active and useful part in opposing the State regulation of vice, and in promoting social purity, devoting much of their leisure time for several years to this work, till it was eventually crowned with success.

The illness which terminated fatally was a long and painful one, but it was borne with very great patience. As weakness increased be frequently expressed his longing for the time when he might be released from suffering, to be "for ever with the Lord."

Robert Foster—1811-1898.
Ann R. Foster—1809-1893.

ANN R. FOSTER was the daughter of Isaac and Deborah Richardson, and was born at Spring Gardens, in 1809. Her father, a man of refinement and intellectual tastes, died when she was only ten months old. Her childhood was one of much indulgence, her health being delicate, and she was kept at home for education. Her only sister died in early womanhood, so that her lot was a secluded one, and passed in close companionship with her mother, to whom she was ever a devoted daughter.

In 1841 Deborah Richardson removed to Summerhill Grove, to be near her two sons, John and Edward. who had settled there.

Records of these early years, dating from 1824, tell of much intellectual activity amongst the young Friends of Newcastle, and of their diligent attendance at Monthly and Quarterly Meetings, going by steamboat and coach, and of

ANN R. FOSTER.

ROBERT FOSTER.

journeys to London; while the constant intercourse with Devonshire and Scotland, introduced an element of much interest and profit into these households.

Her mother's death in 1848 was deeply felt. This loss did but deepen the tie which bound her to her brothers; to whom she was a tender, loving sister, the constant sharer of their joys and sorrows.

As her character developed, the Christian graces of humility and love shone more and more conspicuously. The love of Christ within her brought forth its legitimate fruit of love to man, and in many ways she sought to promote the Redeemer's Kingdom on earth.

Her help on the occasion of a visit to Paris in 1846, for the purpose of distributing New Testaments in that city was truly valuable, and the enterprise was carried out with much zest.

Many charitable institutions received her warm support, the Ragged and Industrial School especially so, from its very commencement. She was liberal to the poor, seeking them out in their dwellings with deep and true-hearted sympathy.

While her heart was thus drawn out in care for others she was always loyal to her own religious Society. She loved the principles of Friends, and sought in a gentle way to instil them. She filled the office of Elder for a long period with much acceptance. She was able to speak the truth in love, and so to manifest her sympathy whilst handing counsel as to avoid giving offence.

In 1858 she was united in marriage with Robert Foster. This did not remove her from her native town: and by it another large circle was added to her own. For thirty-five years this happy union of hand and heart continued.

She was affectionately beloved by her nephews and nieces. Those of the second generation gathered round her as the first had done. She entered into their pursuits with interest; her knowledge of Continental travel, and her acquaintance with modern educational requirements, enabling her to follow the accounts they brought from school and college, at home or abroad.

As the three-score years and ten crept over her a failure of power was perceptible, though her activity continued great.

Early in the spring of 1893 decided signs of weakness appeared, and very gently, day by day, her strength declined till the end came; the end, it may be said, of an uneventful life, yet one of unobtrusive beneficence.

Ellen Richardson—1808-1896.

ELLEN RICHARDSON was born in 1808, and was the daughter of George and Eleanor Richardson, to whose Christian training, example, and prayers, she ever felt she owed very much. She often spoke of her school-days at Ackworth as a time of Spartan discipline; but probably the training received there helped in the formation of her self-reliant character, which, however, made it difficult for her to yield her judgment to that of others, and at times brought her into much conflict and deep searching of heart.

In reviewing her early years she wrote in 1883:—" It was a long time before I came to my Saviour experimentally, as I longed to do, but He *hath* taught me to believe in Him, and in this blessed experimental belief to find rest to my soul.

Family bereavements followed one another in quick succession during her earlier womanhood. In 1840 her brother Isaac died at Ventnor; two years later, after a lingering illness, her only sister, Rachel Pumphrey, passed away at Ackworth; and in 1846 she was bereft of her beloved mother. Thenceforward, for sixteen years, it was her joy to care for and comfort her father, whose bright and useful life was prolonged into his eighty-ninth year.

ELLEN RICHARDSON.

The agitation on behalf of the West Indian slaves found in her a warm supporter. Most of the fugitives who sought refuge in this country from slavery in the Southern States were practically helped by the Friends of Newcastle; and, at her own initiation, warmly aided by her brother and sister, Henry and Anna Richardson, the money was collected wherewith the freedom was purchased of William Wells Brown and Frederick Douglas.

The life work of Ellen Richardson, to which she set her hand only four years after leaving Ackworth School, was the education of the daughters of the working-classes of her native town. "The Royal Jubilee School for Girls" had been commenced by a few practical philanthropists in association with her father, and she was not slow to throw her own energies into its management. This she continued with untiring zeal and patience, until its doors were closed

in 1854. She was not content with guiding the general
arrangements, but she personally assisted in the classes,
especially in Scripture and in reading—two subjects in
which the children particularly excelled. She felt that
upon Bible teaching, and a high standard of moral and
Christian life, much of the success of all educational work
must depend. To the teachers she was an invaluable
helper; and the " Jubilee School " gradually became the
training ground for young teachers, whose studies she
personally superintended. She impressed upon them the
true meaning of education, and would not tolerate any
mere mechanical teaching. Her book, entitled " Principles
of Training," was written under a strong sense of duty,
and she was truly a leader in the elementary education
of girls.

In 1860 "the Schools and Charities Committee" of
the City Council requested her to organise and superintend
their " St. Mary's School "; and for many years the two
institutions were carried on by herself and her lady-
colleagues under similar management.

Cullercoats was the frequent resort of her father and
his family. Here they became warmly interested in the
welfare of the fishermen. They soon found how great was
the need for an infant school, so that the little ones
might be cared for while their mothers were away in the
neighbouring towns selling fish. A school-house was
accordingly built, and it was not long before it developed,
by natural growth, into a general elementary school.

She was diligent in her attendance at meetings for
worship and discipline so long as her strength permitted;
and when confined mostly to her house, her heart often
went up in prayer during meeting time, on behalf of her
friends, and she manifested an earnest interest in the
spiritual life of the congregation.

As the end drew near, a marked mellowing of her
strong character was observable; but her independence

was maintained to the last. During her final illness her sufferings were at times intense ; but through Divine grace she was enabled to bear them patiently, and to feel her Saviour's presence very near. She died on the 26th of fourth month, 1896.

Richard Ball Rutter—1826-1898.

THOUGH Richard B. Rutter had left Newcastle several years before his death, his long association with the city and the circumstances connected with his early ministry may be considered a sufficient warrant for the insertion of this brief notice.

He was the son of Samuel and Elizabeth Rutter, and was born in Bristol in 1826. When he was quite young a love for poetry manifested itself, and being encouraged by his mother to learn pieces by heart, and having an excellent memory, his mind was stored with Scripture and hymns, and this was invaluable to him in later life. On the death of his father, when R. B. Rutter was nineteen years of age, the family removed to Shotley Bridge, and he found employment in a bank at Newcastle.

In 1854, with some other members of the family, he emigrated to Australia, and was furnished with a certificate of membership numerously signed. The rough life of the colony was little suited to his taste, and he returned to Newcastle at the end of two years. Here he made his home for upwards of thirty years, and was again engaged in a bank in the town.

In 1863 he married Anna Maria Clapham, of Newcastle. It seems probable that between the time of his return to England and his marriage he experienced a marked change in his religious life.

In 1860 he believed it right to be baptised with water and to partake of " the Supper," and therefore sent in his resignation of membership with Friends. This was not

RICHARD BALL RUTTER.

accepted; and in after years his opinion on these points was entirely changed. He began to speak in meetings for worship in Newcastle in 1870, and was recorded a Minister in the following year.

Some years later he writes: "My idea of the relative importance of ministerial qualifications is, First, personal piety; second, a call from God; third, deep scriptural knowledge; fourth, personal experience; fifth, sympathy; sixth, hunger for souls; seventh, good sense and tact; eighth, clear speech and free speech; ninth, human learning."

R. B. Rutter was a man of impulsive temperament and much versatility, and the character of his ministry was no doubt influenced by his natural endowments. He often concluded by repeating a hymn in a very impressive manner.

His friend, Thomas Hodgkin, has furnished the following communication: "It is, I suppose, something like twenty-six years ago that our meeting at Newcastle was—I will not say agitated, but—gently swayed to and fro by a proposal to read the Bible in our meetings for worship. Most of the younger generation were in favour of the suggestion, but one or two of our oldest and most esteemed Friends deprecated the change. I need not say that this was not from any want of love for the Bible on their part, but only because they feared lest prearrangement and the institution of a Calendar of Lessons might interfere with the freedom and spirituality of our worship. After two or three meetings and conferences the matter was settled by the withdrawal of the proposal, as the young and middle-aged Friends felt that it would be selfish to press for a change which would evidently be so painful to their elder brethren. We were richly rewarded for this little act of Christian courtesy. I think it was on the next Sunday after the first debate that Richard B. Rutter rose from his seat at the further end of the meeting, and repeated slowly and with deep feeling the magnificent 63rd chapter of

Isaiah:—' Who is this that cometh from Edom with dyed garments from Bozrah?' The effect was most impressive; far more so than any ordinary reading of the chapter: for Richard Rutter was essentially a poet; and, more than most poets, he had studied not merely the composition but the right utterance of poetry. He had a wonderful power of rendering both his own and other men's poetry with the right emphasis and intonation. Thus it was that the glorious poetry of Isaiah seemed to acquire fresh beauty and significance when recited to us on that Sunday morning by our new minister. For some months, I think, he mostly confined himself to the mere repetition of passages, sometimes pretty long passages, of Scripture."

About the year 1880, he retired from business, and they removed to his native city.

He was one of a committee of the Yearly Meeting appointed to visit the meetings of Friends in Ireland, and crossed the Channel several times on this service.

He took a very humble view of his religious attainments, never speaking " as though he has already attained ;" but a growth in grace was undoubtedly experienced as years went on. He was never a strong man, but until about eighteen months before his death he was able to employ himself as usual. The nature of his illness during the last few weeks precluded much expression; but he was preserved in patience and in unfailing trust in his Redeemer to the end.

" Yes, Lord,
How short a prayer may be
It reaches Thee,
Nor hath it far to go ;
And if it seem to rise as incense to the skies,
Yet is its first silent, invisible flow
Downward, Oh Lord,
From Thee
On me :
From the higher to the lower, from the lower to the higher
In one eternal circle runs the heavenly fire."—R. B. Rutter.

ANNA SARAH PROCTER.

Anna Sarah Procter—1845-1898.

ANNA SARAH PROCTER was one of those beautiful characters, who, in the midst of suffering and weakness, bear a wonderful witness to the reality of Christianity.

For the greater part of her life she was confined to her couch, and often in a darkened room. There were periods of very great suffering, and there was always extreme weakness, and at times, intense depression from physical causes. And yet under all these trials, as the years rolled

on, she blossomed into the loveliest and most unselfish of
human beings. To be with her, to know her intimately,
was felt to be a high privilege. Her own pain and
weariness drew her towards the suffering ones, and lying
on her couch, her thoughts turned lovingly to those who
did not possess the home comforts which she had herself,
and thus her active mind originated, organized, and carried
on "The Invalid Loan Society," and the "Fresh Air
Scheme," for the help and healing of the sick and wearied
ones among the poor of this world. In this work her
labours were unwearied and wonderfully blessed. But it
was not to the poor alone that she ministered. It would
be impossible to convey an idea of the extent and depth of
her unselfish thought for others. It seemed to prevade her
whole being. The little children loved her, and rejoiced
over many a pretty gift which just suited them, and which
she selected herself for them. Tired Christian workers
toiling in the cause of suffering humanity, found in her a
most sympathetic friend. She passed on her favourite
books and hymns in the most generous manner, after
having enjoyed them herself, she delighted in sharing them
with others. Many a sorrowful heart was comforted by
her sweet written words. Above all was her touching
humility, and the low estimate she took of herself. Those
who visited her in her bright and airy room, felt the magic
influence of her loving spirit. They knew that it was good
to be with her, that here was one living indeed the Christ-
like life of self-sacrifice and ministering to others; that
there was a reality in her religion, a living power in her
life.

To such whole-hearted disciples as Anna Procter, does
not Christ Himself still say, "Inasmuch as ye have done it
to the least of these My brethren, ye have done it unto
Me."—*Matt. xxv.*

Then spake a shrewd on-looker "Sir," said he,
"I like your picture, but I fain would see
A sketch of what your promised land will be,
When, with electric nerve, and fiery-brained,
With Nature's forces to its chariot chained,
The future grasping, by the past obeyed,
The twentieth century rounds a new decade."

Whittier.

Review.

Contributed by Thomas Pumphrey.

As we have briefly traced, in the foregoing pages, the history and progress of the Society of Friends in this district it may be well to see what we can learn from the study.

The survey shews us that two-and-a-half centuries ago the great aim of George Fox, after he had found "One who could speak to his condition," was "to bring people to Christ and to leave them there." He does not appear to have aimed so much (if at all) at establishing a sect as at raising the plane of religious life in the nation ; reviving the almost buried truth of the direct guidance by the Holy Spirit, in the little as well as the greater affairs of life ; and bringing his hearers under the power of the Spirit of God that they might be re-created into His likeness.

With this object he roused his followers to despise all obstacles and persecution in the prosecution of their Divine Mission. This was the secret of their enthusiasm. Fines and imprisonment could not deter them from their one desire to fulfil their Master's work. When contentions as to dogma "rent and tore the Nation" they met their antagonists with "The Lord hath said."

This direct hostility to the recognized teachers of religion brought them under the arm of the law, hence the charge to "come no more into Newcastle to have any more meetings there at your peril."

But after the passing of "the Act of Toleration" they enjoyed more freedom of worship until, in course of time, they were "hurt by no persecution." Being thus permitted to worship God according to their conscience they settled down into greater quietness and, having acquired a name for uprightness in their transactions in trade, they prospered in business and many grew rich.

There is an old legend that when their opponents found that they could not put them down by persecution they consulted the great Adversary who told them that they were going the wrong way to work; "let them prosper and then they will lose their power." Worldly prosperity has often tended to slacken religious zeal and to deaden spiritual life; and, in degree this was so with the Society of Friends.

They maintained their protests *against* certain customs, such as hat-honour, complimentary titles, fashions in dress and styles of address; but, though there were many noble exceptions, these distinctions became, with some, little more than outward forms from which the vitality had passed away.

It can scarcely be doubted that the importance which was attached to conformity to external requirements withdrew the attention of young people, at a time when their characters were being formed, away from such essentials as the necessity for a change of heart and the transforming power of the Spirit of God, and led many into a false security; into the love of self-indulgent ease, and an undue absorption of the mind in earthly things.

When it was once acknowledged that these external rites were acting prejudicially upon the best interests of the Society, the rein was slackened and some restrictions were removed. Then the pendulum swung too far in the opposite direction; and while the general effect has been salutary in the long run, the tendency has been to lead some away from the guarded sober life which characterized the early Friends.

Happily, alongside of this broader view of things, a wholesome missionary zeal took possession of large numbers of our members. The growth of the Adult School

P

movement, followed by home-evangelization efforts, and then by a revival of Foreign missions, served to furnish incentives to healthy activities which necessarily acted beneficially upon those so engaged. Thus the attention of the Society became less self-centred, and a spirit of Christian altruism was fostered which wrought powerfully for good upon the body at large.

A Friend who attended the Yearly Meeting of the Society in London, after a long interval of absence while these changes had been progressing remarked, with a singular confusion of metaphor, "the stars are set, but the lump is leavened." The speech conveys a suggestive thought, as it tells how the men and women of light and leading, who had been preserved from the deadening influence of formalism, had passed away but that in their places had arisen a galaxy of lesser lights (as it was thought) so that the conduct of business in the Society's parliament was not now confined to a few "around the Clerk's table," but that a wide-spread and lively interest was evident all over the house.

This was only an index of the altered conditions throughout the country, and Newcastle shared in the revival.

The endeavours thus put forth for the good of the masses naturally had the effect in drawing a large accession of men and women into association and membership with the corporate life of the Society. This influx is as welcome as it is natural, but it brings with it some added responsibilities.

These new members must take their due share in the government and discipline, as well as in the work and ministry of the Society; and it is due to these who have not had the advantages of a Quaker training that they should receive, from those who have enjoyed this privilege, that support and guidance which will assist them in the right discharge of their Christian duties.

This is true as regards the character of our Meetings for worship, the right qualification for the exercise of the ministry of the word, as well as in all the varied other ministries which fall upon each member of a Christian congregation.

We need to be on our guard against leading any to depend unduly upon vocal ministry; we need also to watch lest we encourage words without power. Perhaps the best safeguard against both these dangers is the maintenance of a right attitude of spiritual worship as we wait in silence before the Lord.

In these days of rush and hurry, of keen competition and exciting speculation, when

"With electric nerve, and fiery-brained,
With Nature's forces to our chariot chained,"

so much of each day's business is done under high pressure and at express speed, there is perhaps the *greater* need to seek the antidote in the "quiet hour" in the inner chamber or in the silence of our Meetings for worship, when we may be brought again into harmony with the majestic calm, and silent working of the spiritual forces, giving us *rest* in the midst of our activities, and knowing our souls to be at peace with God.

Should we lower the standard which was committed to the early Friends in these and similar respects, we may soon lose the only warrant for our separate existence as a religious community, and the twentieth century may witness another relapse into form without power.

Perhaps we cannot conclude more appropriately than with the significant words lately uttered by the Archbishop of York. They are among many happy evidences of the fact that some of the truths which had been over-laid but which were re-kindled into new effectiveness by George Fox and his followers, are finding more place among some of our sister Churches.

While we rejoice to recognize this, we are more fully persuaded that the Mission of our Society is not yet by any means accomplished, and that the torch which was re-lighted for our predecessors is given to us to take up as they pass away, and to carry aloft as a constant witness to the truth of God.

At the Meeting of Convocation in York Minster, in February, 1899, the Archbishop said he "had been impressed with that feature in the service of the people called Friends, which consisted of spending a considerable time in absolute silence, often, indeed continuing through the whole service. For years he had been under the impression that Churchmen under-rated the blessing and the necessity of silence in public worship. It was true that people often made that feature in the service of the Friends a subject for criticism, and almost for merriment, and said that they met together, sat still, and sometimes went back to their homes without having done anything. The fact was that in waiting upon God in silence they had done a very great deal, and might possibly have received a greater blessing than if they had been occupying the time in uttering their own words addressed to God, or in reading and other acts of worship. It had long been his desire to introduce this feature, where possible, into the services of the Church of England."

Lowly before the Unseen Presence knelt
Each waiting heart, till haply someone felt,
On his moved lips the seal of silence melt.

Or, without spoken words, low breathings stole,
Of a diviner life from soul to soul,
Baptizing in one tender thought the whole.

When shaken hands announced the meeting o'er,
The friendly group still lingered at the door,
Greeting, enquiring, sharing all the store
 Of weekly tidings. * * *

 * * * *　　*Whittier.*

APPENDIX.

Births, Marriages and Burials.

Contributed by John W. Steel and T. Pumphrey.

THE registers of Marriages extend from 1653 to the present time. They may be broadly divided into two classes, those solemnized in private houses and those in the Meeting houses.

Examples may be given:—In 1660, Robert Linton, of South Shields was married to Jane Perrott "in Isabell Larkin's house at North Shields." Similarly Ann Hall, an early Newcastle Friend, was married in a dwelling house to a Stockton Friend; and Thomas Merryman and Mary Neale were united also in a dwelling at Shields, in 1674.

The cause for this class of marriages was simply that the religious meetings of the Society were then often held in dwelling-houses.

George Fox puts his view as to marriage very plainly. He says:—Where, from Genesis to Revelation, did any priest ever marry any? "If priests excommunicate Friends for not being married by a priest, why do they not excommunicate Isaac and Jacob, and Boaz and Ruth, who took one another in the assemblies of the righteous?" And thus he advised that intended marriages should be laid in prospect before the Friends, that the intention should be published by being given notice of at the end of a Meeting; and that on the appointed day the two persons should, in a meeting for worship, "take each other in the presence of at least twelve faithful witnesses." Hence when the meetings were held in private dwellings, marriages took place there after due announcement and enquiry.

. Later, as Meeting houses were acquired, these meetings were held there, and so were the marriages. Thus, John Tizack, of the " Glasshouses, near Newcastle," married, in 1674, Sarah Langford at the Gateshead Meeting house ; and there, in 1687, one of the honoured heads of Newcastle Meeting, Jeremiah Hunter, married Sarah Linton.

So the records run down the centuries ; the marriage that is perhaps the most prominent being that of John Bright and Elizabeth Priestman in 1839, which marriage had also the presence of John and Sophia Pease of Darlington.

The nature of our records and the particulars furnished with regard to marriages are not such as to facilitate exact tabulation.

Some reference has been previously made to the form of declaration of intention and other points regarding the earlier marriages.

Suffice it to say that the number of marriages registered as having been solemnized in the Newcastle Meeting house since 1860, when the altered form of registry came into force, has been only 1·23 per annum. During the early part of this period it was 1·4, and during the latter part only 08·2.

The births recorded were for the former part of the time 4·65 per annum, and for the last few years they have only averaged 3 per annum, or for the whole period of thirty-nine years 4 per annum. The births exceed the deaths in the earlier period, but latterly the balance has been reversed. For the whole period the births have slightly preponderated but only by 0·69.

During the same thirty-nine years the membership has increased by one third but this accession has been more marked in the later years; the average having been as 1 in the earlier period to 4 in the later.

The number of Burials registered since the Friends' graveyard was closed has been 134 or a yearly average of three.

Burials.

Contributed by Thomas Pumphrey.

MENTION has been repeatedly made in the first chapter of the grave-yard in Gateshead as the resting place of the early Friends of this district until the transference of the meeting for worship from Powell's Court to the premises in Pilgrim Street.

The original registers were long ago removed to Somerset House; but the copy of these earliest records, which is kept in the safe at Newcastle gives, not only the burials in the Gateshead ground but all,—whether in Gateshead or Newcastle,—which had taken place prior to 1777. The exact position of only a few of these interments is given; but the earliest which is stated to have been in the burial ground in Newcastle is dated 5 mo: 15-1698. The register is prefaced thus:—

"The Register Book of the Burials of the People of God, in scorn called Quakers and others their relations and kindred, who have been buried in their burying ground in Gateshead in the county of Durham, 1660 to 1776."

This further preface is added:—

"The above book, together with the book containing A Register of the Marriages of the People of God in scorn called Quakers in and about the Town of Newcastle and of Gateshead in the County of Durham $\frac{1688}{1689}$ to 1776. Also the Register of Births from 1662 to 1777, were by direction of Newcastle and Benfieldside Preparative Meeting sent to the care of William

Manley, London, to be at the disposal of the meeting for sufferings 12 mo. 2, 1840."

At the conclusion of the entries there is this footnote :—

"1777 Third month. The Monthly Meeting registers being now kept at Newcastle it is judged unnecessary to keep up this Particular Meetings record as long as the Monthly Meetings record is kept here."

Following this first book of death registers is a copy from the certified schedule in the hands of the Recording Clerk in London from 1776 to 1823. It is followed by a careful register kept by James Gilpin, dating from 1823 to 1854, when the ground in Pilgrim Street was closed. This is the only period in which the exact positions of the graves are indicated : these are shewn by numbers corresponding to the figures affixed to the grave-yard walls; but this index is only given to seventy-five ; twenty are described as "at the East End,"— mostly young children,—or as having been buried away from Newcastle. Fifty-nine interments, included in James Gilpin's records, took place in the Westgate Hill General Cemetery, and three at Jesmond, between the years 1830 and 1854, when the Friends' grave-yard was closed.

A plan in the register-book, a framed copy of which is on view at the Meeting-house, gives the names of the 75 graves; but it is clear that these are but a small proportion of the burials in the Pilgrim Street yard. (See appendix, page 219).

Assuming that only one-half of those in the earliest register were buried here, we have 124
and adding those from 1776 to 1823 229
and these 75, together with the 12
not indicated 87

we may assume that the total number
was not fewer than 440

The various schedules may be thus summarised :

	Registr.	Dates.	Period.	Entries.	Average per ann.
Gateshead......	1	1660 to 1698	38 years.	86	2·53
Gateshead and Newcastle...	1	1698 to 1776	78 ,,	246	3·15
Newcastle......	2	1776 to 1823	47 ,,	229	4·85
do,	3	1823 to 1854	31 .,	158	5·10
do.	4	1854 to 1899 in public cemeteries.	45 ,.		

These figures may lead to the supposition that the congregation has nearly doubled in size between the first and the later periods. Regret is sometimes expressed, and perhaps oftener felt, that the interments in our grave-yards are not marked by inscribed stones or even by raised mounds.

The propriety of erecting such tablets was discussed in the Yearly Meeting of 1825, and liberty was given to Preparative Meetings to allow them at discretion, if desired.

Accordingly the minutes tell us that at Shields and at Sunderland such permission was exercised, but the following was the judgment of Friends of Newcastle :—

Report and Minute of Committee—

REPORT.—" To the Preparative Meeting. Agreeable to appointment we have met, and recommend the size of the stones for the Newcastle grave-yard to be 1 foot 8 inches by 2 feet 6 inches and 6 inches thick, and of Heworth stone. We also propose that Edward Richardson and Daniel Oliver be nominated as the Friends to whom applications shall be made by parties desirous of having a grave-stone over any grave.

     Signed,

JOHN RICHARDSON.   WILLIAM HOLMES.

DANIEL OLIVER.   ROBERT WILSON.

Newcastle, 6 . 11 . '50."   WILLIAM TAYLOR.

Copy of a Minute of Newcastle Preparative Meeting, held 12 / 1 mo. / 1851 :—

" The subject of grave stones, referred back to this meeting, has again claimed our consideration ; and it is agreed that in each case the friends of the deceased who apply for stones, refund the cost to the Friends appointed to superintend the placing of them."

FREDK. CLARK,

Clerk."

Though liberty was thus granted, it has not been availed of by any single family. Possibly the deterring cause may have been that it has been found almost impossible to prevent the ground from being over-run by neighbouring children when the gates are open during the occupation of the school and mission rooms.

The accompanying plans, with reference numbers and record of names, dates of death and ages (for which see Appendix, page 219) will, therefore, be of more value in the absence of any entablature *in situ*.

The closing of inter-mural burying-places took effect, by Government orders, in 1854; but prior to this date the Westgate Hill General Cemetery had been opened and used by Friends as early as 9th Month, 1830.

The Jesmond General Cemetery and, at later dates, those provided by the various Parish Boards, notably, that of Elswick, have been the resting-places for the dead chosen by Friends in recent years, and tomb-stones have been erected without restriction in common with other denominations. Thus was broken down another of those marks of exclusiveness which distinguished our predecessors in life as well as in burial.

Names of Friends
Buried in the Grave-yard, Pilgrim Street,
as shewn on Plan.

No, on Plan.	Name.	Date.	Age.
1	Sarah Rooke	1839 ...	62
2	James Beezon	1830 ...	78
3	Mary and Thomas Gowland	1830 ...	3 3m.
4	Isabella Burt	1830 ...	0 7m.
5	Deborah Richardson	1848 ...	75
6	Thomas Arundale	1828 ...	30
7	Hannah Watson	1828 ...	17
8	Thomas Burt	1828 ...	64
9	Eliza Gilpin and William Watson ...	1829	1y. 4m., & 2 y.
10	Mary Bragg	1828 ...	30
11	Ann Wilson (N. M.)	1828 ...	68
12	David Sutton	1829 ..	92
13	Timothy Cutforth	1829 ...	42
14	Rachel Burt	1825 ...	16
15	Mary Cutforth	1825 ...	10
16	William Graham	1826 ...	0 2m.
17	Jane Robson	1826 ...	10
18	Margaret Sutton	1827 ...	78
19	Robert Foster (Northumberland St.) ...	1827 ...	74
20	Ann Grey	1827 ...	54
21	Ann King	1827 ...	69
22	Sarah Goundry	1823 ...	6
23	John Brantingham	1823 ...	45
24	Robert Foster (N.M.)	1823 ...	71
25	Mary Ann Burt	1823 ...	24
26	Isabel Hudson	1823 ...	79
27	Thomas Salter	1824 ...	1 10m.
28	Jane Dixon	1824 ...	77
29	T. H. Pattinson	1824 ...	2
30	Marian Rooke	1846 ...	38
31	Rachel Priestman	1842 ...	20
32	Margaret Bragg	1840 ...	79
33	Eleanor Richardson	1846 ...	68
34	George Richardson	1862 ...	89
35	Joseph Richardson	1848 ...	—

No. on Plan.	Name.					Date.		Age.
36	Ann Piele	...	...	...	...	1852	...	88
37	George Bell	...	...	...	...	1848	...	59
38	Child of W. W. Pattinson	...	...	...		—	...	—
39	Margaret Pattinson	...	...	...	...	1842	...	27
40	Rachel Pattinson	...	...	...	...	1850	...	59
41	Anne Piele	...	...	...	...	1841	...	36
42	William Tessimond	...	...	...	...	1844	...	30
43	John Watson	...	...	...	...	1852	...	71
44	Mary Oliver	...	...	...	...	1842	...	77
45	Daniel Oliver	...	...	...	...	1848	...	77
46	Henry Broadhead	...	...	...	...	1842	...	24
47	Hannah Watson	...	...	...	...	1850	...	84
48	Elizabeth Hunter	...	...		..	1835	...	84
49	Elizabeth Watson	...	...	...	...	1837	...	15
50	Sarah Morton		...	...	...	1838	...	23
51	Robert Watson	...	..	...	...	1840	...	22
52	Joseph Watson (Holly Hill)		...	...	...	1840	...	86
53	Joseph Watson (W. W's. son)		...	...	...	1840	...	16
54	Ann Watson	...	...	...	...	1849	...	72
55	Margaret Cutforth	...	...	...	...	1834	...	45
56	Rebecca Richardson	...	...	...	...	1834	...	27
57	Hannah Chapman	..	...	...	...	1840	...	73
58	Thomas Oliver	...	...	...	...	1834	...	1 10m.
59	Emily Esther Priestman	...	...	...	...	1834	...	0 10m.
60	Isaac Watson	...	...	...	...	1835	...	18
61	Margaret Foster	...	...	...	...	1835	...	78
62	Mary Ann Oliver	..	...	...	...	1835	...	4
63	Jonathan Wilson	...	...	...	...	1832	...	25
64	John Cutforth	...	...	...	...	1833	...	16
65	Child of James Wall	...	...	...	...	—	...	—
66	Ann Baimbridge	...	...	...	...	1833	...	60
67	Anne King	...	...	...	...	1834	...	78
68	Jane Watson	..	...	...	...	1848	...	61
69	Jane Sutton	...	...	...	...	1850	...	57
70	Rachel Watson	...	...	...	...	1831	...	5
71	Charles Bernard Gilpin	...	...	...	...	1831	...	0 10m.
72	Joseph Arundale	...	...	...	...	1831	...	58
73	Catherine Rawlinson		...	...	....	1832	...	—
74	Mary Ann Salter	...	...	...	...	1832	...	31
75	Jacob Tessimond	...	...	...	...	1832	...	24

Joseph John Gurney
at Brunswick Place Chapel.

EXTRACT from a letter from George Richardson to his wife, dated

" Newcastle, 8th mo. 6th, 1830.

My Dear Eleanor,

* . * * * * *

A public Anti-Slavery Meeting is to be held in the Meeting House, at Brunswick Place, on Fourth-day next at twelve o'clock, when that celebrated advocate of the enslaved African (and for the welfare of the human family generally,) Henry Brougham, is expected to speak. We also expect Joseph Hughes at the Anniversary of the Bible Society, in Friends' Meeting House, on Sixth-day evening.

It is concluded to postpone the Monthly Meeting one week, to permit Friends of Newcastle to attend the Anti-Slavery Meeting, to which Sunderland and Shields Friends have agreed.

Joseph John Gurney and his Mary got in to a three o'clock dinner from Sunderland yesterday, at Summerhill. I told thee of the Public Meeting to be held in our Meeting house. Some apprehensions being entertained that it would prove too small, the Methodists were sounded through the medium of George Bargate, to know how far it would be agreeable to them for the Meeting to be held in Brunswick Place. The result was favourable to the step, and notices were printed for the occasion and distributed by the doorkeepers. It was thought about 1200 people attended, and it proved a solid, instructive and good meeting.

J. J. Gurney stood up with that exhortation of Christ, " Search the Scriptures " etc., and was enabled beautifully to explain the various proofs of the Divine origin of the Holy Scriptures, and to enforce a diligent and meditative perusal of them. No other book has so opened and revealed the nature of the Almighty Creator of the universe, or so clearly explained His wonderful attributes ; His power, His omnipresence, His goodness, but most especially (that wonderful attribute which belongs to Deity alone), His prescience, a power of foretelling future events ; thereby proving that the world is upheld by His discretion, and governed after the counsel of His holy will.

This opened the way for J. J. G., to dwell largely on Prophecy, and to repeat many of the most remarkable relative to the blessed Redeemer; afterwards shewing their wonderfully exact fulfilment in Him: the whole was beautifully illustrated so as to confute the infidel, or the vain philosophy of men who rely solely on their own reasoning powers. He also earnestly enforced the practical application of these solemn and important truths to the improvement of the heart and the amendment of the life.

* * * * * * *

At Meeting this morning our dear friend had excellent service. In his testimony he explained and enforced a larger number of the * Testimonies of Friends than I ever before listened to at one time, and in so clear, instructive and impressive manner as must have made a deep impression on many minds. His communication was especially directed to the youth. The meeting was remarkably full to be on a week-day.

They set off soon after Meeting, hoping to reach Belford this evening.

Thine in true affection,
GEO. RICHARDSON."

---

* See " Observations on the Distinguishing Views and Practices of the Society of Friends," by Joseph John Gurney, 1842, and other works explanatory of the Doctrine, Practice and Discipline of Friends, which may be obtained on loan from the Libraries at their Meeting-houses, on introduction by a member of the Society.

The Queries, 1845.

"THIS meeting feels a lively concern to remind our members that the intention of directing sundry queries to be **answered**, relative to the conduct of individuals in the several branches of our Christian profession, is not only to be informed of the state of our meetings, but also to impress on the minds of friends a profitable examination of themselves, how far they act consistently with their religious principles." * * * * *

EXTRACT FROM THE BOOK OF DISCIPLINE, 1787-1833.

"The first twelve are to be answered in writing to the Spring Quarterly Meetings, and from thence to the Yearly Meeting. The 1st, 3rd, 10th, 13th to 18th, are to be answered in writing to the Quarterly Meetings in Autumn; and the 1st and 3rd to the Quarterly Meetings in Winter."

i.—Are meetings for worship and discipline kept up, and do friends attend them duly, and at the time appointed; and do they avoid all unbecoming behaviour therein?

ii.—Is there among you any growth in the truth?

iii.—Are friends preserved in love one towards another; if differences arise, is due care taken speedily to end them; and are friends careful to avoid and discourage tale-bearing and detraction?

iv.—Do friends endeavour by example and precept to train up their children, servants, and those under their care, in a religious life and conversation, consistent with our Christian profession; and in plainness of speech, behaviour and apparel?

v.—Is it the care of all friends to be frequent in reading the Holy Scriptures; and do those who have children, servants, and others under their care, train them up in the practice of this religious duty?

vi.—Are friends just in their dealings, and punctual in fulfilling their engagements?

vii.—Do friends avoid all vain sports and places of diversion, gaming, all unnecessary frequenting of taverns and other public-houses, excess in drinking, and other intemperance?

viii.—Are friends faithful in bearing our Christian testimony against receiving or paying tithes, rent-charge in lieu of tithes, priests' demands, and those called church-rates?

ix.—Are friends faithful in our testimony against bearing arms and being in any manner concerned in the militia, in privateers or armed vessels, or dealing in prize-goods?

x. Are the necessities of the poor among you properly inspected and relieved; and is good care taken of the education of their offspring?

xi.—Is due care taken, when anything appears to require it, that the rules of our discipline be timely and impartially put in practice?

xii.—Is there any appearance of convincement among you, and have any been joined to our Society on that ground since last year?

xiii.—Is care taken early to admonish such as appear inclined to marry in a manner contrary to the rules of our Society; and in due time to deal with such as persist in refusing to take counsel?

xiv.—Have you two or more faithful friends, appointed by the Monthly Meeting, as overseers in each particular Meeting; are the rules respecting removals duly observed, and are the general ADVICES read as directed?

xv.—Are friends annually advised to keep correct and clear accounts, and carefully to inspect the state of their affairs once in the year; also to make their wills and settle their outward affairs in time of health?

xvi.—Are friends clear of defrauding the Queen of her customs, duties and excise, and of using or dealing in goods suspected to be run?

xvii.—Do you keep a record of the prosecutions and sufferings of your members; is due care taken to register all marriages, and to record on the minutes of the Monthly Meeting all births and burials; and are the lists of your members revised and corrected once in the year?

xviii.—Are the titles of your Meeting-houses, burial-grounds, &c., duly preserved and recorded; are the rules respecting trust property observed; and are all legacies and donations properly secured and duly applied?

R. ROBINSON AND CO. LTD., PRINTERS, NEWCASTLE-ON-TYNE.